CW01460461

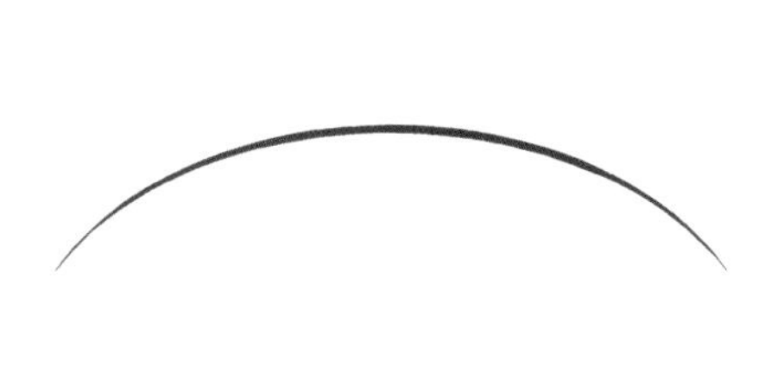

DAWN

A Fresh Perspective on Life, Death, and the Other Side

. . .

Thoughts on the afterlife based on my mom's deathbed insights

by Dorie Burdett Pickle

This book is dedicated to my mom.

This is your book, Mom.

I am just following your lead.

Dawn: A Fresh Perspective on Life, Death, and the Other Side

Published & Printed: integ
Austin, Texas

ISBN 979-8-218-34481-8 (First Edition 2024)

Cover background painting by Dorie Pickle
Book layout and design by Kim Karrasch
Chapter illustrations by Diane Tyler

CONTENTS

FOREWORD

Since the dawn of humankind, THE two big questions each of us grapple with are: What is our purpose in life? And what happens after it ends?

Such is the moral of Dorie's story in this book. Its universal relatability is in the inescapable understanding we all have that our parents' inevitable passing will teach us something about our own. Will their assurances and beliefs hold true as they face the great unknown? How can we comfort them? How can they comfort us? Why is something so commonplace and expected still so mysterious and daunting?

Dawn illuminates this journey we all face with a powerful retelling of the final days of one woman's life as observed by and told by her daughter. If you have watched a loved one pass away, you know that it is a transformative experience that exposes you to greater truths—bigger than any one life or any one belief system.

And whether you interpret Carlie's visions as something divine, sublime, or simply one's way of coping, this book invites you to trust in and honor the experience of a loved one facing death. Furthermore, Dawn demonstrates the power of setting aside fear and expectations for something more hopeful—possibility.

Dorie's journey recounted herein reminds us that we can never be sure what a new day will bring. If you're willing to be open to messages from the other side, I assure you that her experiences will help you get a little more comfortable with the unknown and the fate that we all will someday face.

– **David Wyatt**, Communicator and friend

PROLOGUE

My mom asked me to write this book while she was on her deathbed. It is a responsibility that I could not ignore. I think no one could. So I'm passing this along not only to fulfill that obligation, but also to honor the life she led, the lessons she taught me, and the beautiful end-of-life visions she had during her last few days.

I am noting direct quotes from her in *blue italics* so I can be confident that I am not putting words in her mouth. Out of respect for her, I want to be clear in distinguishing between what was from her directly, and what I am extracting and exploring from there.

This is my story of caring for my mom as she passed away, her powerful and compelling insights as she approached death, and my surprising spiritual journey with her since then.

. . .

My mom, Carlie Sue Burdett Hunter, died on August 1, 2019, at the age of 73. Her physical body had fallen to kidney disease and complications from pneumonia. We were always very close—we collaborated on creative projects, consulted each other on our paths, and helped each other laugh and cry our way through life's trials. She was the best mom I could have asked for, and I still miss her every single day. She had come close to dying from a similar (and related) disease when I was a kid, so her death was a loss I had expected and feared for most of my life.

Before July 29, 2019, I was not a very spiritual person, and I believed that having any real knowledge of the afterlife was impossible. I thought that death was maybe final—the end of the line. I thought that any insights into the *other side* were unknowable. I had come to terms with being comfortable with those unknowns decades ago. I did not believe in ghosts, spirits, angels, or other supernatural phenomena. I was maybe open to those things conceptually, but I didn't *believe* in them.

Since the age of 19, I had believed only in what science could *prove*. I considered myself *agnostic*—not claiming to know about these matters one way or another, and I felt comfortable with those unknowns. I had accepted long ago that I would never know what lies beyond this life.

...

But the events that occurred on and after July 29, 2019, have convinced me otherwise.

...

My mom was a kind, smart, considerate, genuine, and compassionate person who loved Willie Nelson, University of Texas Longhorns football, *National Geographic,* and any kind of chocolate. She was a composer, a musician, and a poet. She loved math, travel, history, and family. She was a devout Christian, attending her non-denominational church weekly, volunteering and singing in the choir, playing the piano for funerals, and bringing food for group events.

Before the very end of her life, she didn't talk much about her thoughts about the afterlife with me other than the occasional Christian-based references to Heaven and Hell.

During those precious last days I spent with her, while she was passing away, my mom had powerful visions and dreams of the afterlife, the Universe, and our spiritual place in all of it. I listened as she emphatically proclaimed and described to me what she witnessed while at death's door. She insisted that I write and publish a book about it, a book called *Dawn*—this book.

. . .

After she passed, I experienced several acute and specific signs from her. These signs and her visions have blown my mind and exploded my understanding of our spiritual and eternal reality.

Before these events, my mother and I were in different worlds spiritually speaking. She went to church, and I didn't. She believed in an afterlife, and I wasn't so sure. I had stopped praying years ago; she prayed and meditated many times a day.

We didn't talk about spirituality too much, although I knew she still prayed for me and my eternal salvation. Thankfully, with our relationship in mind, she didn't press me on it too much; she always trusted that I had love in my heart, and that would have to be good enough.

After the events I witnessed as she passed and after having experienced her spiritual presence since then, I have a new and profound sense of calmness and acceptance of life and death. I have found a new joy that is deeper than I knew could exist before. I find more pleasure in small things and in connection to others than I used to. I laugh more. I cry more. I am a changed person.

Through all of these experiences, I have come to believe in spirits, eternal life, reincarnation, and the possibility of communication with the dead. I believe that karma is real. I believe that death is a simple transition on a much longer journey than any of us has ever imagined. I believe that death is not to be feared.

I believe our ancestors are guiding us from higher realms. I believe we can access or at least grow closer to these other realms by exploring our dream life, accessing different levels of consciousness, and leaning in on our innate creativity. I believe we are all connected; all life forms, from all of history and into the future, are connected in a very real and important way. And I think that the stars and the morning dawn play mystical and important roles in all of it.

(Oh, and I also have come to believe that time is vertical, not horizontal as it is so often depicted.)

How did I come to believe these things?

Let me explain.

A LARGER JOURNEY

My phone rang on a Monday morning earlier than I had expected. It was my dad. I answered immediately, hoping the report from the hospital would be good news. It was not.

My mom had been admitted to the hospital with pneumonia about a week earlier. She had been the recipient of a kidney from my dad 16 years ago and her transplanted kidney had recently shown signs of decline. The lifespan of a transplanted kidney is limited, so we all feared she was living on borrowed time. But she'd been doing so well in recent years. Generally, she stayed active and worked hard to maintain a healthy lifestyle.

She kept meticulous notes about her various medications and managed all of them impressively. Because of her transplanted kidney, she went into the hospital more frequently than the average person when she got sick with the flu, a urinary tract infection, or another malady. To be honest, I was used to the frequency of her visits to the hospital, so I hadn't been too concerned about her most recent admission for pneumonia. But this time, it was starting to feel a little different.

...

Dad said that she was talking on and on about visions and dying, and he asked me to come right away. I packed and said goodbye to my husband, Ben, and our kids, Henry and George. I did my best to check out of work and headed an hour and a half north to the hospital.

When I arrived, I urged my dad to leave my mom's room and take a break. A devout and supportive partner of more than 50 years, Dad had been by her side for 48 hours straight in the ICU without having slept much. I hugged him goodbye and recommended he try to get some sleep. I promised I would take over for a day or two.

...

As I was settling into the room, my mom couldn't stop talking about the visions she was having. She seemed to have a new understanding of life, death, and how it all works; how it's all connected. She said she could see it all so clearly now that she was nearing the end of her life. She seemed inspired rather than scared. I found her receptive attitude comforting and concerning all at the same time.

She was focused on my writing, drawing, and understanding the experiences she was dictating to me. I listened, I typed, I sketched, and I nodded. She started talking about it to anyone—including the food crew, the cleaning staff, the nurses, and the doctors—who entered the room.

She would tell them in an excited and confident voice, *"I wish you could see what I have seen!"*

Hospital life went on as normal around us with all its beeps and bustling while she danced in the space between life and death. And I witnessed.

. . .

She described how she'd been having visions and dreams about this for months, but that just that morning, she had seen *all of it.* And she wanted to see it more; she was ready to go.

"I am on the threshold of life and death. ***At the end, you can see all of it,*** *and it makes so much sense,"* she said. *"I am ready to go.* ***There is nothing to be afraid of."***

She described it to me the best that she could: the shape of it, how it all relates to itself, to us, and the grander scheme of things. I encouraged her to keep downloading it all to me, and she asked me to take notes.

She was giddy that I didn't think she was delusional; that I would listen to her, and I would take her seriously. She was so excited to have someone willing to engage with her on the topics of death and the other side.

Many people are dismissive when someone starts talking about such ethereal things. A lot of people just want to move on to more mundane, "normal," or less sad, scary topics. But my favorite college course 20 years ago was a religious studies class called "Modern and Ancient Death Rituals," so I guess I've always been a little bit curious and open to talking about death and the afterlife.

She had been up most of the early morning trying to record her revelations on her phone and telling anyone who would listen. For months, she had been dreaming and writing about these feelings and visions through poetry and song. She had even mentioned to my dad weeks in advance that the end was getting near for her, and she could feel it coming. Finally, she was getting her revelations out and onto paper, offloading the burden and excitement onto me.

She continued to describe her insights to me, trying to capture these surreal and otherworldly visions in human terms, in English words. I continued to listen, write, and sketch.

She was enraptured with her new vantage point. Standing on a cliff, overlooking the ledge between life and death, she was hovering in the space between this world and the next, whispering to me about its very nature.

I took it all in.

. . .

Mom said:

> *I've had a series of dreams over the past several weeks leading to one big vision last night and this morning where I saw all of it.* ***At the end, you can see all of it.***
>
> *I've had intense visions of large groups of people. Women in headdresses with children, and hordes of people, so many people moving in large masses across the globe. Trillions of people, and I'm one of them. These visions are helping me realize that we are a part of this larger journey, and I'm no longer afraid to die.* ***I'm a part of the energy.***

"It is a much larger journey than I had ever thought," she said as she looked at me with shining, bright eyes—ecstatic at this revelation. She had been talking for hours, but she caught my attention with that one. We both paused.

All week long I've been awake most nights having dreams and visions with hordes of people, moving and swaying together; walking. In some of the visions, men were on horseback. Several visions were not good. Many people were in distress, shivering masses, in burned-out cities, and bloody children were crying. Someone tries to help a hurt child, and someone shoots that person and grabs the child. Things like that. Terrible visions.

. . .

She paused and took a deep breath. Trying to recover from such awful thoughts, she closed her eyes and centered her mind.

I had another vision of a beautiful hillside full of green trees and family groups sitting here and there together and on some scattered benches—like a big memorial park. Groups of schoolchildren sitting on the grass, then getting up and leaving. Like an ongoing memorial service where people were coming to pay tribute.

She opened her eyes and continued, holding her hand out steady in front of her as if to show emphasis on what she was about to say, *"But it's also more personal than that. I think it's also the coming of the end of my life."*

She continued, *"I'm looking at big issues here. Do you understand? The biggest issue; the issue of life and death.* ***I am facing death. I am at the threshold as we are speaking."***

SHAPES IN THE CLOUDS

My mom continued to hold my attention throughout the morning and insisted that I take note of everything she was seeing and saying. I did my best. She was increasingly enthusiastic about these visions. Although she was physically exhausted, sick, and tired, she also had an air of excitement about her, mixed with a readiness for relief from her physical pain and suffering.

She was ready to join with this larger Force she kept describing. She was enticed by it. She seemed to want to step through to the other side, with her eyes wide open, like a child entering Disney World for the first time.

I was worried and scared at this talk of death; I did not want her to die. But I felt like it was so important to her to discuss it that I tried my best to push my feelings aside and keep up with her descriptions of these new, enticing things she was experiencing.

Having been through chemotherapy in the 1980s, a partial colectomy and dialysis in the 1990s, and a kidney transplant in 2003, she was familiar with death's door. She had faced it before. She had made her peace with dying. She didn't try to hide from the reality of it, and she tried to live in a way that allowed her to feel at peace with it—physically, spiritually, and mentally. To that end, she made an active effort to appreciate life each day she could by taking in the small things, being in the now, especially when she was feeling good and had her health.

...

At some point during our intermittent conversations about these grand and other-worldly topics, she shifted to a different angle.

"Do you see shapes in things? Like shapes of objects in the clouds, or faces of things in a wood grain pattern?" she asked me. *"Yes, all the time!"* I said. And we talked a bit about some of the abstract things in which we see shapes or images; for me, in my shower tile; for her, in her living room rug.

She believed that this skill, along with a spirit of openness, could lead to a capacity to garner something greater than the obvious, deeper than the surface of what we know about our existential journey. She insisted that this skill or instinct was underlying an ability to understand the Universe, the afterlife, and our collective and individual place in all of it.

She emphasized that the ability to see shapes in the clouds—the specific kind of imagination work that takes—employs the brain in a way that is important to understanding the "beyond." She believed it was using the mind in the same way she was using it now to see things from this new perspective. She said that this "seeing-the-shapes-in-the-clouds" creative skill would be required for a human to be able to understand the bigger picture—the "30,000-foot view"—of our spiritual reality.

. . .

While we were discussing this, her main doctor came in to review the results of some of the tests. Her kidney numbers weren't looking very good. He described the various implications of these results, while a nurse across the room prepped more medicine and worked with various machines. The doctor's news was not positive.

Mom interrupted the doctor to ask if he sees shapes in the clouds. *"Do you know what I mean? Do you see objects or shapes in abstract patterns?"*

He glanced at me, like, *"Did she not hear the bad news I'm delivering?"*

"Yes, I used to see shapes in the wood grain of my dad's carpentry work. I used to help him in his woodshop when I was a kid," the doctor responded, compliantly. Mom nodded and glanced at me, like *"he might get it."* She winked. She seemed skeptical but also comforted that he might be able to understand some of the things she was witnessing.

Regardless, his news about her kidney function and overall direction was not good. His report was discouraging, and he urged us to prepare for the reality of emergency dialysis very soon. She didn't seem too bothered by it though. *"Those were the medical facts about my body, now let's get back to discussing what really matters"* seemed to be her approach.

I was getting very concerned, and I told her that we would need to have a serious conversation about whether to do dialysis sooner rather than later. This was a decision she did not want to have to discuss. She did not want to do dialysis again.

She turned the conversation back to seeing shapes in the clouds. She said that this ability was indicative of being able to understand some of the concepts about the structure of the Universe and how we fit into it.

She insisted that our ability to use our imagination—to be able to employ our creativity— was indicative of being able to comprehend the structure of our collective experience together, beyond our current understanding, beyond our current physical and sensorial limitations.

She said, *"Seeing these things is a sign of being able to understand—to see this reality for what it is."*

NO TIME FOR LUNCH

Constantly interrupted by various medical procedures—blood draws, vitals, breathing treatments, meds, and visits from doctors—we eventually got back to business. I tried to get her to eat, but she pushed aside lunch more than once. She said that we didn't have time for that. She wanted to focus our time together on downloading all of this to me. *"You are writing this down, right?"* she asked me a few times to make sure I was taking it seriously. This was of critical importance to her.

That night she talked about the "other side" and how she was ready to go. She was at peace with it now that she understood the larger journey. I listened and comforted her. But I thought she would recover—*she just needed the will to live,* I thought. To me, the medical facts didn't seem to indicate that she would pass away. Plus, there was always the dialysis option. PLUS plus, she was in such good shape in all other ways as far as I knew. She took really good care of her health, except for the occasional KFC indulgence on a bad day.

I believed that she could live with these new-found spiritual truths, passing them along with a passion to others; be inspired by them; write music about them, and write the book called *Dawn* that she kept describing to me in detail.

I told her that writing *Dawn* could be something she worked on during dialysis after she got out of the hospital. It could be her new mission. I was hopeful even though she seemed so certain that she was already transitioning to the next world, whatever that was.

. . .

The doctor came in around 8:30 the next morning and informed us that her kidney creatinine level was at 5.4 and that she would need emergency dialysis within the next 24 to 48 hours to survive and be able to recover from pneumonia.

During this discussion about dialysis and other options, she said that her body wanted to go. She told my dad that she wanted to go. He begged her not to go. She looked at him and said that she was very, very sorry. She said that she loved him so much, but that it was her time to go. Watching this, my heart began to break, slowly widening at the fault lines.

. . .

Right about that time, nurses came in for more tests and my dad headed into the hallway. I watched him edge toward the door as his eyes and shoulders slumped toward the ground. I saw a tall and proud man facing the rest of his life without his partner of more than 50 years, without his life-long best friend. He loved her and was not nearly done loving her.

Our big strong rock of a man suddenly seemed like a pebble under the shadow of a large and looming wave.

I followed him out into the hallway and hugged him. Looking him in the eye, I told him that it's not about us anymore, it's not about him anymore. *"It's about her now. This is her journey. And, she says it's her time to go. I'm so sorry,"* I said gravely.

. . .

Meanwhile, I knew this was what she felt emotionally and spiritually, but as far as I knew, there wasn't a medical reason why she couldn't come through this and recover.

So, while I wanted to respect her will to follow her spirit to the other side, my dad and I, as well as her doctors, felt that if her blood was cleaned out by dialysis, she might feel differently. We still held on to hope.

She had been in the hospital for more than a week now. She was tired and sick. Plus, she had been battling kidney disease for more than 40 years. Of course she felt like moving on– that was understandable.

. . .

But I, of course, didn't want her to go. I wanted her to see my children grow up, and to be here for me like she always had been. I wanted her to ask me about my day, and give me advice about which tile to pick for the bathroom remodel or which dress to choose for a big event. I wanted 30 more years of advice about life, love, marriage, and children. I wanted her to keep telling me how I needed to use more wrinkle cream. I needed her to bug me to keep exercising and eating vegetables and drinking less alcohol. I wanted her to keep listening to and laughing at my crazy stories, giving me the best advice, sending the world's longest texts, and always, somehow, knowing the exact right thing to say. I wanted her to stay here. I wanted her to keep being my mom.

I started to feel a little overwhelmed. So, I took one of my standard walks around the hospital grounds, considering the situation, and trying to wrap my head around what was happening. I decided to come up with a three-part plan to save her. If all else fails, I'm always a fan of a good three-part plan.

Step #1. Get her outside somehow so she could see the sky and feel the sun on her body. Possibly try to move her to a brighter, better room with the sky in view.

Step #2. Lift her spirits by entertaining and distracting her, make her laugh with memories, jokes, and photos; help her stay connected to her people.

Step #3. Focus all other energy on her recovery. I felt like the sooner she started feeling better physically, the more these visions of dying (and maybe death itself) would subside.

I returned from my walk with my new plan and was motivated to try to shift things, slowly but surely. *"Give it the old college try"* as my mom would say.

I tried to convince her that even though she had seen these visions and was at peace with dying now, that didn't mean that death was *imminent*.

Not being afraid of death is not the same as having a death wish. I emphasized to her that this knowledge did not mean that she had to die on this go-around in the hospital. I thought she could recover from pneumonia, get dialysis, and live many more years.

. . .

The room she was in was so small and dark—no sky, no sunshine. Tucked away in a far back corner of the third floor of the hospital, she hadn't been outside or had even seen the sun or the sky in more than a week. I felt compelled to try to get her moved to a brighter room where she could see the sky, feel the sun on her cheeks, and have hope. I wanted her to stay connected. I wanted her to stay here...in this world...with us. I asked the nurses to see if there was a possibility of moving her to a brighter room. I hoped part 1 of my plan was possibly underway.

To activate part 2 of my plan, I texted my husband, Ben, and asked him to send photos of the kids and anything else he could think of to make her laugh and raise her spirits.

While we waited to hear from Ben and the nurses, I thought it might energize her if we could go listen to the self-playing piano in the lobby of the hospital. She was a talented and passionate pianist and composer, so I thought maybe this would trigger something in her that was required to keep going, to stay *here*.

At my mention of going to see the piano, mom looked like she might cry.

This made me think she still loved music but was having a hard time reconciling her passion for music with dying. The look on her face was of sad homesickness; like she was taking one last look over her shoulder at the wonderful parts of her life—the precious moments, the perfect chords, and the magic-filled melodies.

I asked the doctors if I could get her in a wheelchair and take her down to see the piano, get some sunshine, and maybe even watch the sunset with me across the parking lot. Maybe one of those things would spark something in her to give her the strength to recover and the will to live.

Something.

Anything...

I felt desperate.

...

But there ended up not being time for any of that. She reluctantly agreed to do two rounds of dialysis just hours before her blood pressure fell rapidly which led to a quick decline; and despite the intervention, she landed in the ICU in a medically induced coma.

We didn't have the opportunity for any further discussion in person about the matters of seeing shapes in the clouds, the Universe, or the connection between this world and whatever lies beyond.

She was right. There had been no time for lunch.

Flashback to 1986 / Amarillo, Texas

It is unusual that the garage door is open and my mom's car is gone and my dad's car is there. Just...abnormal.

Usually, when I get home from school, the garage door is closed. Usually, I walk home from school past the Gregorys' house, through the empty lot, down the alley, and through the backyard past the closed garage door. Usually, my mom is at home, the house is bright, and there are snacks and greetings. But not today.

I scoot past the ping-pong table and open the garage door into the house by the utility room. Why is my dad's car at home in the middle of a weekday? Why isn't he at work? And where is my mom's car? It is eerie.

I walk into the dark house, and I can instantly feel that no one is home. It is too still, silent in fact.

I see blood on the floor. The blood draws a line from the garage door into the kitchen. I call for my mom with a shaky voice while I instinctively follow the trail of blood like it's the yellow brick road, a clue to some end.

Silence. Sounds of the air conditioner blowing. I call for them—"Mom?" pause. "Dad?" pause. Air conditioning.

The bloody path leads me to the kitchen table where I see a note addressed to me:

Dorie—

Mom has to go to the hospital—the special one in Temple. Call your friend Sharon Moser See if you can spend the night with her. Everything will be fine. We will call when we can.

Love, Dad

. . .

I pick up the kitchen phone and immediately dial Sharon's phone number. I wind the long curly phone cord around my hands with nervous energy. Cord winding. Phone ringing. Cord winding. Phone ringing.

"Hello, Moser residence..."

Sharon lives across town and is my best friend from the last school I attended before we moved a few months ago in the summer between the 4th and 5th grades. I don't have any friends in my new neighborhood yet. I fidget with the curls of the phone cord and wrap them around my fingers while I explain the blood and the note I found.

"Dad! We have to go get Dorie!" Sharon yells and hangs up without saying goodbye. We are both frantic and kind of half-crying.

I pack a bag and wait by the front door. I'm not sure how to lock up, but that seems trivial and silly, so I just don't.

While waiting, I notice that dark clouds are gathering and that the sky looms gray — heavy, and low. It's getting increasingly dark like it's nighttime, but it's only 4 p.m. Finally, they arrive.

After quick hugs, I climb awkwardly into the back seat of the large white suburban. By the time we get to the end of our block, the sky is billowing and black. It's spitting rain angrily but only a little at a time.

We speed across town, going faster than

legally allowed, trying to beat the storm. It begins hailing.

I look out the window and I see a tornado forming in the skies on the horizon a few miles west of us. Its recognizable light gray wiggly funnel silhouette stands out brightly against the black thunderhead clouds.

It looks like the crooked, bony finger of a giant witch, dipping down through the clouds to swipe the ground—just for fun.

We go faster.

The tornado scrambles my thoughts of my mom and the blood and my darkest fears. The tornado is angry—twisted and lost—ambling about, spreading destruction needlessly. It feels like I'm controlling the weather—like the weather is a mirror of my emotions. It feels right, and I am glad there is a tornado.

The funnel aches toward the ground like a giant anteater sticking its long nose through the clouds for a quick snack. It comes down like it's always been up there—just waiting for the cloud cover to reach down and take what it wants.

. . .

We make it safely to the Mosers' house and my dad calls to say they have made it to the hospital, and the parents talk and arrange for me to stay with the Mosers for several days.

They report that on their way to the airport when they were trying to get to the hospital, they had a flat tire (during the tornado, no less). A perfect stranger picked had them up and delivered them to the airport.

Later that night, the storms clear away and the stars come out.

Mom recovers slowly over the course of a few months via love, medicine, and miracles. And I return to skipping home from school to her greeting me at the back door with snacks and questions about my day.

SAND THROUGH OUR FINGERS

We were hopeful that the dialysis treatment would be successful, and the medical staff said they had stopped some internal bleeding they had discovered. She was intubated and as unconscious as they could make her to keep her comfortable.

That night, Ben, Dad, and I ate dinner at the hotel across the street from the hospital with my sister, Bliss. She had rushed there from across the country where she had been camping off-grid in the deep woods of Montana. She had hiked each day to a nearby peak where she could get cell service to check in on mom. She had offered to come much sooner. Until now, I'd been telling her I thought Mom would be OK and to stay on her trip. But we both agreed that intubation sounded pretty freaking serious, and Bliss was on the next plane to Austin.

After dinner, my sister spent the night in her sleeping bag next to Mom in the ICU.

As I went to bed that evening, I struggled with not being able to talk to Mom. I didn't know if she would make it through the night. But I felt so hopeful she might be OK.

Throughout the night, Bliss reported that the ICU nurses and doctors worked tirelessly to put in a central line and do some other procedures. Even the doctor with the super fancy shoes had worked hard on her—he really seemed to know what was what.

But early the next morning, Bliss texted and said to come to the hospital right away. Mom's internal bleeding was continuing to get worse. The hospital staff couldn't do the second dialysis treatment because of her blood loss. The transfusions, now up to the seventh one, also had to stop.

The only way to determine what was causing her continued decline and try to stop the internal bleeding more successfully would be invasive surgery, which she probably wouldn't survive. We all agreed, and Dad signed the paperwork to not do anything further that was invasive, as Mom would have wanted. We were grateful that she had made her wishes clear before her decline.

The decision was made. We called our brother, Shannon, who was already en route from up north. He was coming as fast as he could considering how quickly things had become serious, but he said not to wait on him. He didn't want her to suffer any longer than necessary, especially not on his account. The doctors removed all the equipment that was supporting her breathing and turned off various machines except for essential monitors.

. . .

We sat with her for five long, surreal hours listening over and over to her piano music - recordings of songs she had written about and for each of us over the years. We gathered around my mom, brushed her hair, and put Aquaphor healing ointment on her lips. We told old stories, we laughed, and we cried. We held hands, we held each other, and we waited. We listened, we prayed, and we witnessed.

. . .

It was taking longer than any of us had expected—although who knows what to expect in these situations. At one point, I lightly joked that she was probably waiting for the right song to come on to let go.

Her breathing was slow and getting slower.

The pastor from my parents' church came to say the Lord's Prayer. We held hands and cried. An hour or so later, the hospital's chaplain came by and prayed with us, delivering her to

God. Then, a song mom wrote for herself years ago called "My Song" came on. Unexpectedly (to me at least), Dad leaned down and kissed Mom lightly on the lips right before she exhaled her last breath.

. . .

It seemed like she had slipped away from us like sand through our fingers; each medical possibility failing while we and her medical team desperately tried to hold on to her. But each grain of silky sand quickly followed the one before, and pretty soon we were staring into empty palms, wondering how this had possibly happened.

It was obvious when she had left her physical body. To me though, somehow, it seemed now like she was not gone, but rather, was...*everywhere*. This feeling was unexpected and surprising to me.

. . .

We said goodbye. We gathered our things and her things, and we walked out of the hospital to our cars in a state of shock, and one person short.

We drove to my parents' home about 45 minutes south of the hospital and started making phone calls. Ben bought groceries, made dinner, and cared for all of us—keeping the food and the drinks flowing. Our brother, Shannon, arrived. We communed on the back patio around a candle, a single point of light, as we talked into the night.

A new reality began to settle in; it was the beginning of a new era.

THE WAY IT WORKS

*"**At the end, you can see all of it,** and it makes so much sense."*

So, what was it all about? What were Mom's visions of the Universe and our place in it that brought her so much enthusiasm and hope in her last few days?

I will do my best to lay it out here exactly as she described it to me.

*"I have seen it—the way it works. It's a special shape. It's like a tornado—but it's not a violent thing like a tornado. **It's a thing that builds and grows,**"* she said, directing me while I sketched on paper and then made a crude mock-up in Photoshop.

She was giving me edits and inputs to make it reflect a skeletal version of what she was seeing.

From her new vantage point, she could now discern and describe to me that we were part of a larger ongoing journey with hierarchical levels structured in a tornadic shape, like this:

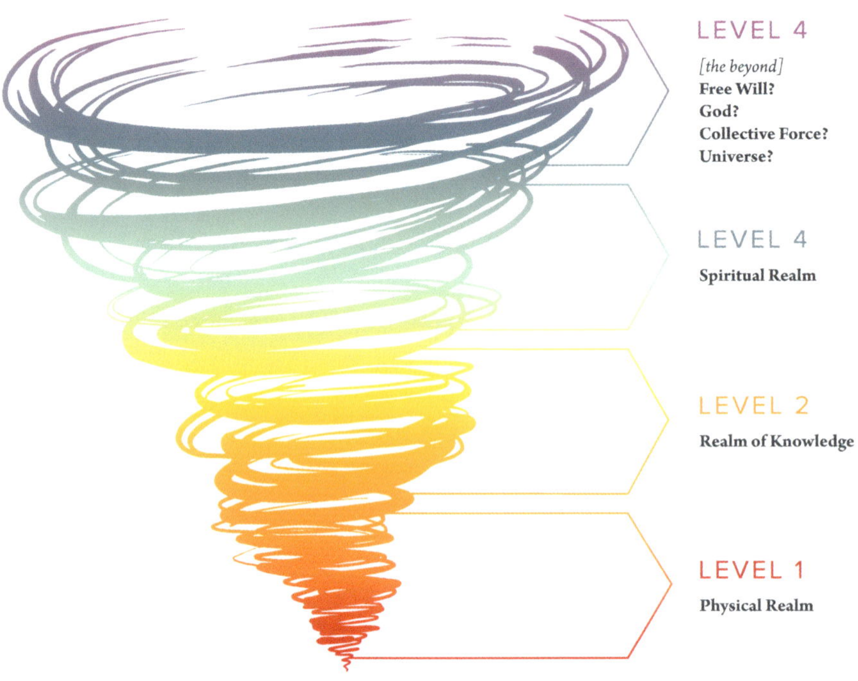

Please note: This is an abstract representation of the ideas Mom described and it doesn't imply precision. There are probably a million artistic ways her vision could be showcased and interpreted.

According to her description, there are four basic levels to this funnel-like structure:

> *We live in the bottom level, which is the physical realm. The next level above physical is knowledge, above that, the spiritual realm, and finally...I'm not sure what to call it....Will or God, maybe. There isn't a word for it.*

We talked about each level and this is my understanding from our limited conversations:

Level 1 – ***The Physical World****:* This is the bottom level at the base of the structure. This level is the physical world that we live in while we are inside of a physical body requiring air, water, and bread. On this level, we scrounge for food, enjoy fine wine, and suffer from arthritis. On this level, we blow out birthday candles, hold a child's hand, and suffer through chemotherapy and war. This level is full of loss and suffering, but also, beauty and triumph. This level is about survival and achieving health.

Level 2 – ***The Realm of Knowledge****:* This is the level where we learn and grow in how we understand the Universe, the stars, the planets, nature, and our place in the world. This level is all about education and comprehension. This level is intellectual and open to learning. At this level, we ask questions and get answers. This level is about growth and wisdom. At this level, we build our knowledge on top of the bedrock of knowledge that has come before us. Our ancestors and the entire history of humanity have built a stockpile of knowledge—this is where we add to it. This is where we use it to reach higher heights.

Level 3 – ***The Spiritual Realm****:* This is the level where we have a connection to the universe and nature. This level requires the breath of life, the bread of life, and the water of life. This level is about love, emotional depth, and a deepening connection to us, the natural world, and other beings and spirits. This level is about the Force within us becoming stronger and more evident. This is our Jedi training.

Level 4 – [***the beyond***]*:* Mom didn't have a word for this level other than maybe the word "Will." But neither the word Will nor the word God fits. She said it was a level that didn't have an easy-to-define name or a word in English for it. She said that words didn't apply to it. When she was describing it to me, she was tongue-tied at the idea of having to assign it a label.

This level is final, infinite, ever-changing, and growing. This level is about freedom and choice. This level holds influence. This level is hard to comprehend. This level is the goal, the ultimate, the Universe. For purposes of discussion in this book, I will refer to this level as [*the beyond*] with brackets and italics to continually recognize that this term is a placeholder because there is no word that can capture its nature.

In those precious moments in the hospital, we talked quite a bit about its specific shape. Mom wanted to be very clear that it was like a tornado or a funnel, spiraling upward. She seemed fascinated by it like it was a dazzling sight to see. It seemed to entrance her. She spent quite a bit of time trying to describe it to me in detail.

She didn't say the word reincarnation, but it seemed clear from our conversations that it would require multiple "lives" to get from the bottom to the higher realms—maybe even millions of lives. She implied that this spiral structure is the shape of our spiritual reality, and it's a long journey of lessons being learned over and over as we make progress up the structure toward [*the beyond*].

It was unclear to me from our conversation if "you" are a physical human only in the physical realm or if it is possible to be in a physical body on the other levels. It was clear in Level 1 you are in a physical body. And she made it clear on Level 4 you are energy or a spirit, definitely not in a physical body, or at least not restricted to one specific physical body. But we did not discuss where that transition from physical to non-physical takes place along the course of one's journey.

According to her visions, it is *not* possible to know which level you are on at any given point, at least not while you are still a unique individual or a physical human if I understood it correctly.

. . .

As I've been digesting this vision of hers over the past couple of years, I've been considering this structure and how we move through it upward, making progress up toward [*the beyond*]. How are we supposed to advance through the levels?

In my mom's last few months, she was thinking a lot about the concepts of echoes and ripples on a pond. With these themes, as with the spiral structure, there is a common element of building and growing. If we are advancing vertically through the structure, we are growing on top of our lineage, building on what each generation (or previous lives) before us started. We, and those who came before us, are all one story, one continuum. Each generation builds on the one before, leading us upward one day at a time.

While on her last trip with my dad that summer and the 10 days in the hospital upon their return, she wrote about the generational echoes through our lives. I found this on her phone after she had passed.

Memories of beloved friends, of loved ones, are never gone. The energy of life is never lost. It sends echoes on through our lives like ripples from tossing a pebble into a pond or a coin into a fountain. The ripples form circles that spread and grow. As we pass them on, they flow down through the waters (fabric) of time; they double back and spread again. The energy of life is never lost.

Their songs reverberate through our lives, singing over the meaningless clatter, ringing and giving meaning through the dust of ordinary life. They are echoes of life, echoes of love.

Toss a coin into a fountain. It makes circles that double back and spread again. Its energy is never lost. May these memories live forever!

Their melodious sounds amplify each other in harmony—and the piercing, clashing sounds echo as well, as each note sounds its true voice, in a splendidly organized dissonance that intensifies the whole. As they rise upward together in lovely abandon toward the Great dome of heaven. The sweet sounds and the bitter blend in sublime disunity, resulting in the lifting up of our hearts upward.

Because she focused so much on the concept of echoes and ripples in her last few months, I've been thinking about it and paying attention to things along those lines. When we celebrated my in-laws' 50th wedding anniversary, they talked about sharing lessons they learned from their parents and how we all pass along their examples of love, passions, interests, and values.

I think my mom's point was that we see ripple effects of those in our lives, our families, and our roots. We are a continuum of their stories.

Maybe it is the same with us as we work our way, one life at a time, up through this structure, through the various levels that my mom described. Maybe we are the collective energy of our ancestors or past lives; we are cumulatively adding new rings to the same tree; adding ripples on the pond, echoes of our past, building toward the future on the foundation of the generations that came before us.

If that is the case, then the biggest question becomes, "How"? How do we work our way up, how do we make progress?

If I understand my mom's visions the way I think she meant them, I think the answer is pretty simple. We must try.

We must try to be and do better. We must try to learn the lessons of love and life from our ancestors. We must address and repair (or at least try to repair) things that are broken from the generation before us. We must fix what isn't working. We must make improvements along the way, keep learning, keep listening, and keep trying.

With all of this in mind, I've started thinking of time as a vertical concept, not horizontal as most timelines show and how most of us discuss it. Each lifetime builds one tiny rung at a time, building upward.

As I digest this vision and reflect on it, taking it all in over the past four years since Mom died, it continues to make more and more sense to me. Everything I consider seems to fall into place somehow when I think about this possibly being a reality.

TO EACH THEIR OWN PATH

Mom not only talked about the tornadic shape of it, but she also discussed the ways we ascend through the various levels. She eagerly tried to describe the process to me.

"An individual within this funnel, this structure of levels, everyone, every human being, has a certain route through—a certain path they will take to progress upward."

I found this message very comforting when Mom expressed it and I still do. She went on to describe that as each soul travels up through this structure, progress is made at various rates and through various forms—transitioning between phases and making progress upward through many lifetimes and different forms of life.

Each of these levels is hard work—each level possibly requires many lifetimes, and many lessons learned over and over in a large variety of ways.

All individuals will progress upward naturally as a part of the overall network. But according to her visions, multiple paths can help you go from one level to the next—like tunnels going upward between the levels. These various paths serve as conduits between the levels toward [*the beyond*].

. . .

If I understand correctly, she indicated that individual "souls" age and learn as they move through the various levels as part of the collective. Older souls know how to lead and progress because they have been on the journey longer and are connected to and understand the energy of the structure.

Mom said that these older souls, like Jesus or Buddha, can serve as guides, charting a path by which other individuals may follow, elevating themselves in the process. She said that others do not follow guides, and take more individually led paths, like spending time in pursuit of betterment, nature, art, or musical interests that are native to the structure itself.

According to her visions, these are not just direct paths that are unrelated or disconnected from each other; they are not exclusive. An individual can move upward using various paths to get between the levels, choosing the path that works best for them at the time, the same way two people climbing a tree may use different branches to reach the same crown.

. . .

Do you know that email messages are split into bits and bytes and that those bits travel separately on their own across the Internet? They go through different states and nations and servers—individually! Not the email as a whole—it doesn't stay together as a whole item as it travels. Each bit has 8 bytes and the head byte knows where it's going and leads the other 7 bytes via whatever pathway it deems to be the most efficient route for it, using its discretion to find the best journey to its destination.

They take different paths to arrive at the same destination based on many variables—speed, traffic, bandwidth, outages, and all sorts of conditions. For example, part of an email might go through servers in Tennessee, while other parts of it travel through Iceland and back. They make these determinations based on what each head byte finds to be the most efficient path. Then, when the recipient opens it, all the individual bits of an email message arrive at their destination and re-form, regrouping into one big, whole email again.

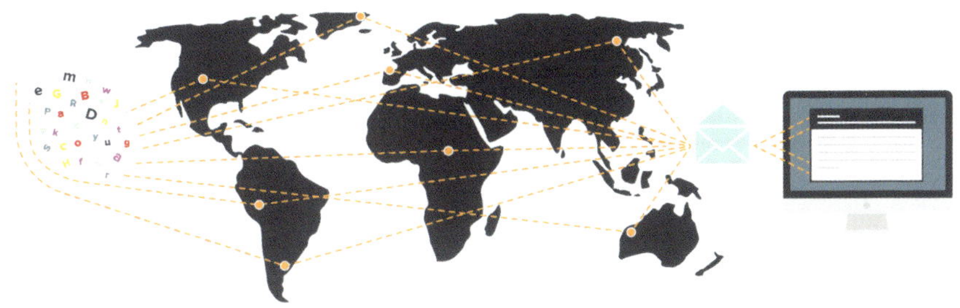

Consider the way water flows through a watershed. Tributaries branch off, and creeks rise and fall, but all of the water flows toward the ocean, taking various pathways to inevitably get there. Each drop of water falls or rises where it may, traveling with a group toward a larger group, merging and melding into one—flowing toward a goal—a release, an opening, the water droplets slowly but surely combining to become a collective force.

The way my mom described how it works is similar in concept to the way these systems work. Our beings advance up through the levels—spiraling and climbing up these pathways. Energy elevates and progresses upward through the levels using any of these routes. Each individual must choose or create a path that works best for them—whatever is the most efficient and effective path upward for that individual. But we are all striving and constantly progressing toward a collective unity—toward the same inbox, the same ocean made of rivers—a collective *oneness.*

Mom described that the way striving upward works best is for people to take the path that makes the most sense to them. You might even take multiple, different paths upward at different times. The journey is fueled by striving toward progress, toward advancement upward.

We are here to awaken from the illusion of our separateness.

– Thích Nhất Hạnh

. . .

Paul Kalanithi, a dedicated and talented young surgeon, was cut down in his prime by colon cancer. During the last few months of his life, he wrote a book called *When Breath Becomes Air*[1]. In it, he talks about the yearning, the striving that we naturally crave when we are engaging in life. *"The defining characteristic of the organism is **striving**. Describing life otherwise was like painting a tiger without stripes*[2]*."*

This is the front of the card my parents gave to me for graduation. It remains on my desk to this day.

. . .

The paths my mom took were: following Jesus Christ and his example, staying in close touch with nature, immersing herself in music, and taking time to serve and love her family and friends. She clung to these pathways like ropes in a jungle, using them to climb up through life's challenges, through the sickness, through the pain, through the beauty and the miraculousness of life. She fueled the climb by the love and connection she saw and felt between them, from them, and because of them.

Along the paths that people take, according to my mom's visions, there is constant interaction, a constant connection to the Forces around you, and the other energies that are moving alongside you up through the funnel. Knowledge and love all grow stronger as more and more souls learn, grow, strive, and build the future together. We build and build on the bedrock of history, each of us on a path upward following various Forces that we find on our way to help guide us through.

...

After experiencing a rough day in the hospital toward the end of her life, Mom was nodding off when one of the nurses took over for a new shift. I commented on how organized this new nurse was.

"Look, Mom! Corina's setting up everything she'll need overnight so you can get some good sleep. She's so organized. She's the King of the nurses!" I was joking around and being a little silly (and very sleep deprived).

To my and the nurse's surprise, Mom sat straight up in the bed and all of a sudden, she was alert and upright. Boldly and with a very strong voice she said, *"Corina is NOT the King. GOD is the King!"*

At that point, Corina and I each raised a single eyebrow and looked at each other, like, *"Oh snap!"* And Mom continued, after slowly narrowing her eyes on Corina—looking right into her very soul it seemed. The room froze—it seemed like time stood still while we waited to see what she would say next. *"Corina is a Force!"* she said joyfully and sternly at the same time, her eyes lighting up.

"Welllll...that's coooooool...," I said in a kind of a sing-song voice, breaking the tension and looking sideways at Corina. "Yeah, Corina is a Force!" I said. Corina smiled and agreed confidently that she was and definitely had always been a Force. Mom relaxed back into bed with a smile, and Corina and I laughed at the drama and relief of the interaction.

...

So what is a Force? Has my mom just seen too many *Star Wars* movies?

Perhaps. But the concept of a person being a Force is not new or foreign. We see them in our communities. We see them in our churches and synagogues, we see them on boards of directors, we see them in nursing homes, and we see them in our schools. These "Forces" are people who are willing to give their time and energy to help others around them and to make a difference in others' lives for the better, even if it's at their own inconvenience or expense.

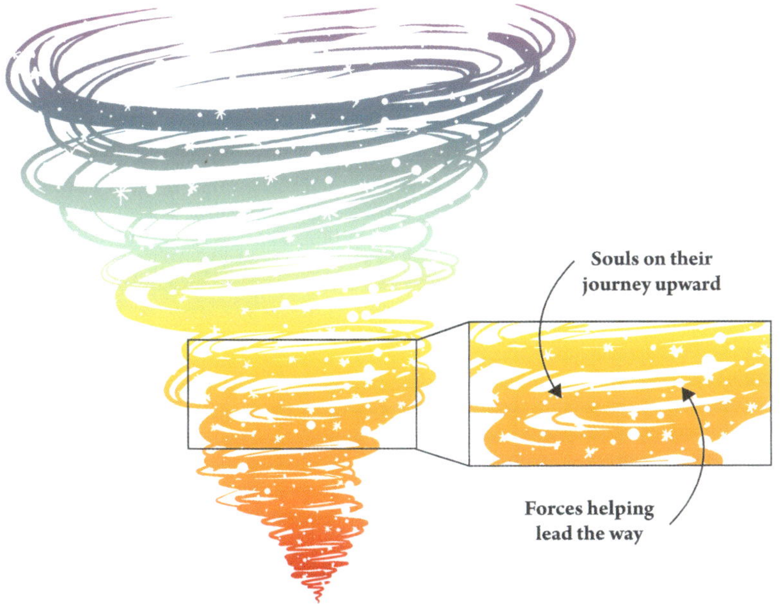

According to Mom's visions of how things work, these Forces help lead us. They help us advance and move upward through the structure. These can be people in our families or people we seek out. We intuitively seek Forces that guide us efficiently upward through the structure. But we have to listen to our intuition, our gut instincts.

When I was a teenager, my mom emphasized the importance of the friends I made. The people you choose to be close with are the people who will have the most influence over you, so, choose people you admire and seek out people that you can aspire to be like, she would say.

When we choose people with whom to spend time, we are choosing our Forces and our guides that will lead us to the paths we will follow. This is one of the most important choices we will make in our lifetimes.

. . .

I know it's corny, but since my mom died, I've been binging a bunch of shows that weave grief into their themes. One thing I heard really resonated with me. In the Season 2 finale of *This is Us*, the character Randall said:

> *Those of you who know me, know that I'm big on control. It's taken me years to accept the fact that there's absolutely zero point in trying to control the future. 'Cause nobody knows where we'll be. Not even a year from now. But...what we can control are the people we choose. Choosing our people is the closest we come to controlling our destiny. Because...while everything else may change, if you choose right, your people will stay the same. Whether that's tonight or a year from now, or 10 years from now.*[3]

THE GRAND CYCLE

One of the main things my mom talked about when describing her visions of the structure was its shape, which seemed to be of critical importance to her. So, I've been thinking a lot about the shape of what she described to me.

My older son, Henry, was obsessed with the Fibonacci sequence when he was a young kid. He has always been into math and the Fibonacci sequence fascinated him.

If you aren't familiar with it, here is how it works:

> *The Fibonacci sequence starts like this: 0, 1, 1, 2, 3, 5, 8, 13, 21, 34, 55, and so on forever. Each number is the sum of the two numbers that precede it. It's a simple pattern, but it appears to be a kind of built-in numbering system for the cosmos.*[4]

The sequence has kind of a magical quality to it:

> *The golden ratio is sometimes called the "divine proportion" because of its frequency in the natural world. The number of petals on a flower,*

> *for instance, will often be a Fibonacci number. The seeds of sunflowers and pinecones twist in opposing spirals of Fibonacci numbers. Even the sides of an unpeeled banana will usually be a Fibonacci number—and the number of ridges on a peeled banana will usually be a larger Fibonacci number.*[5]

Isn't it interesting that there is this numerical pattern that flows through so many parts of our universe?

All these things found in nature follow this same pattern:

- Flower petals
- Seed heads
- Pinecones
- Fruits and vegetables
- Tree branches
- Shells
- Spiral galaxies
- Hurricanes
- Faces
- Fingers
- Animal bodies [including human]

- Animal flight patterns
- The uterus
- DNA molecules

So, as you can see, this is a fundamental shape of our existence and how things are built. And it *just so happens* that it's very similar to the shape of a spiral my mom described to me. Mom said that this spiral-shaped cone connects all of us while we are at various levels. If you looked at the tornadic structure in my mom's visions from above, might it also follow the golden ratio?

What if this pattern, this numerical and fascinating mystery, is also the shape of our collective "larger journey" that my mom was describing?

Wouldn't it make sense that the larger structure of our existence might flow and mimic that same shape? Wouldn't it make sense, then, that it follows the same golden ratio? But maybe we can't see it because we are a part of it. Maybe we can't see it because we *are* it.

BREADCRUMBS

I'm not a superstitious or religious person. Despite how my interest in this subject matter may paint me, I'm practical and logical.

But since my mom passed, the strangest things have been happening. I have had dozens of specific, very powerful signs from her that make me feel confident that she is still looking after me and still communicating with me in some strange new ways that I don't fully understand. These experiences—these "signs" from her—have been so surprising that I have been compelled to share them with family and friends, and now, here with you. These experiences could just be coincidences, but that is not what I have come to believe.

. . .

The day after she passed, we were all heartbroken. I had been personally caring for her for several days in the hospital, so I was both physically and emotionally exhausted. When I returned home the next morning, I felt lost.

I wasn't sure which way was up and which way was down, which direction was right or left. I woke up and cleaned the house and ate something. I made tea. I unpacked my bag from the hospital. I cried. I started the laundry. I fed the cat. I cried. I did the dishes, and I cried some more.

At some point mid-morning, even though it was a dreadful 100 degrees outside in the Texas heat, I felt the need to run. I ran my normal route, relieved that neither my emotions nor the heat forced me to stop and cry or throw up or something along the way. I ended my run at my favorite place in the whole world—a local spring-fed pool called Barton Springs—to find respite from the heat and garner some solace.

I dove into the cold springs and, relieved from the heat, climbed out and sat on the half-wall next to the pool. I looked into the clear green waters, just staring for several minutes, expressionless, thinking about my mom.

Entranced, I thought about what an amazing woman she was, and how I still felt close to her. I pondered on how I didn't feel devastated. I felt more stunned than anything. I still felt like she was all around me, that she was there with me, more than ever. I could feel her presence. She was not gone.

This feeling—this connection—was unexpected. I had left my interest in the spirit world behind long ago around the age of 18, when I left my childhood church.

Still staring into the waters, thinking of her specifically, I was surprised when a woman came and sat directly between me and the pool. The pool was not crowded, she could have gone to a million other places. But before changing my gaze, I noticed that right there on the back of her arm, directly in my line of sight, was a tattoo of a little chubby chickadee, looking right at me. The bird's eyes stared right into my line of sight without my moving an inch or changing my gaze.

Here's the thing: My mom's favorite little bird was a chickadee. Her little salt and pepper shakers? Chickadees. Her album artwork on her CD? Chickadees. The main imagery on her website? Chickadees. She just really loved them and surrounded herself with them in a variety of ways. Chickadees are bright-eyed and bushy-tailed, just like my mom. It was kind of like her spirit animal.

When I suddenly found myself face to face with a chickadee just as I was thinking of my connection to my mom, the message felt palpable. It felt like a real true connection to her. I felt like that little bird was looking directly at me, saying, *"Good job. Way to get out there. Way not to cry in bed all day. Do this. Take these steps. Yes, keep going. Put one foot in front of the other. You are doing this. This is hard, and you are doing it."*

I realize that that's a lot for a tattooed bird to say. They don't normally speak, at least not at length like that.

I felt the message sink in. I felt it as clear as a sunny day at Barton Springs Pool. It was unexpected, bizarrely comforting, and surprisingly spiritual. I was reading supernatural things into a normal situation, I realize. But the message seemed so clear at the time. I hadn't experienced anything quite like it ever before in my 44 years.

...

The next day, we were planning the burial. Mom hadn't wanted a funeral with her body on display and we were all in such a state of shock, so Dad decided on a very private graveside burial with just our immediate family to be followed by a larger memorial service a few days later with friends and family, with enough time for people to plan and travel.

I wasn't sure what arrangements, if any, my dad had made for the graveside service, but I knew there wasn't much of an official program. Considering my mom's passion, I felt strongly we couldn't put her in the ground without any music.

She always loved when Ben played the Beatles' song *"Blackbird"* on his guitar. Every time we were together as a family, she would ask him to play it for her. It's beautiful, and they had a special bond over music (in addition to science, history, and cooking). So I asked him if he would be willing to play it on his guitar while they were lowering Mom's body into the ground at the graveside service. He agreed and, while a little reluctant with nerves, he knew it would honor her in a way that she would have truly loved.

About an hour after this conversation with Ben, my good friend Holly came by to pick me up to go get a pedicure. Some self-care and a chat with a close friend were what I needed. Plus, my mom was always on me about neglecting my toenails. I'd rather not bury her with the half-polished, half-grown-out, half-scratched-off situation I had going on.

We went to a specific salon across town because I had a gift certificate that was about to expire. We chose our nail color and our names were called. Two seconds after we settled into the bulky pedicure massage chairs, a guitar version of *"Blackbird"* came on the speakers. I kid you not.

My jaw dropped. I told Holly about the connection, and I texted Ben to recount the story, *"I think Mom approves,"* I said. He agreed.

. . .

It was so strange. It felt so much like she was communicating with me in these direct ways. I found it a little eerie, definitely bizarre, but also very comforting at the same time. I welcomed it and yearned for more signs.

Surprised and excited in a new and unexpected way, I was slowly realizing that although her physical body had passed away, she was not gone.

. . .

Every few days or weeks I would have something happen that felt like a sign. There have been dozens of them. And, the more I think about them and talk about them, the more people I run into who have had very similar experiences. Things that, from all accounts, *feel like so much more* than just strange coincidences.

I started thinking of these signs as messages, little "bread-crumbs," if you will, from the other side. They seem like little guideposts for me to follow, leading to what exactly, I don't know. They seem to pop up when I need encouragement or love, or guidance in some specific way.

. . .

When I was a kid, I was told to have faith—to believe. And I tried so hard. I did. But I had too many unanswered questions. There were too many holes in the stories. I didn't have *actual* faith no matter how much the church or my parents told me to or wanted me to. I didn't believe it. But now, having shared these experiences with her as she neared death, and receiving these ongoing signs from her, I can say that I have *actual faith*. I *believe* that there is something; that there is a *"beyond."*

...

Six months after we buried Mom, I made an appointment with her doctor to give him some of her music and thank him for all they had done to care for her. It was hard to return to the hospital (the place where *it* happened), but I felt strongly that I needed to follow up in some way. I couldn't leave things so open-ended with the person who tried so hard to save her. And, I felt like I needed to face the hospital where I had cried and struggled and feared and lost.

I intentionally waited six months to have time for the rawness of it all to subside a bit, but not so much time that I could not remember everything clearly.

As I walked in, the sounds and smells were all too familiar. Facing my old temporary home, I entered the front doors by the information station with an elderly volunteer. I walked down the big hall lined with donor names. And I passed through the long windowed room with the peaceful artwork of landscapes near and far.

Walking the same halls that I walked during those days of hope and caretaking, I also passed by the bench where I had openly wept in the prayer garden on the afternoon when I realized we could lose her.

I walked past the player piano that I had wanted to take my mom to see in her last days. It was playing all by itself as usual, without a human player. A ghost-like performance with the self-playing keys, it had the mechanics down but without any of the passion or the hard-earned skill. It sounded beautiful but was somehow unimpressive.

...

My meeting with the doctor went well. We talked about what went right, about what went wrong, and about how we both missed my mom. He loved getting her music CDs I brought for him, and we had a great conversation about how medicine needs to constantly evolve. I secretly hoped something would be learned through this loss.

We hugged and I thanked him for all the care he had given my mom and my family during the whole ordeal and over the years.

...

I left the hospital the same way I came—passing the crying bench in the prayer garden, back through the corridor of donors, and past the self-playing piano. But this time, for the first time I'd ever seen in the decades of visiting this hospital, an actual person— an elderly man with a gentle touch and next-level skills—was playing the piano.

Surprised by this, I caught his eye between the piano base and the raised lid, and we had just a moment there where we connected. I was so happy to hear a live performer on this usually human-less machine.

I walked away down the long hall and was about to exit the building into the rainy parking lot when I stopped in my tracks. I turned around and walked quickly back toward the piano.

I couldn't believe it when I heard the pianist start to play *"It is Well with My Soul"*—my mom's very favorite old hymn. I knew it was her favorite because she had written and played an arrangement of it in recent years and she had told me how much she loved it.

The lyrics themselves contained quite a message of approval and contentment—*"It is Well with My Soul."*

Once again, I felt a strong sign directly from her—from the other side, from the beyond. She approved. She was glad I had come. It all was *well with her soul.*

...

When I got back home, I was so relieved to have had the conversation with the doctor, I crawled into bed. It was a cold and rainy day, so getting into a dark, cozy bedroom was just what I needed. I put on my favorite yoga pants, climbed under the covers, and turned on the TV.

While I was waiting for it to boot up, I was thinking about how strange it was that the pianist was playing *"It is Well with My Soul."* Not only was it her favorite hymn, but it also contained such a clear message in the title itself. It truly felt like a sign directly from her from the other side. This shit was starting to hit home.

As I was thinking about this, I turned the TV on and the word "SIGNS" was in big white letters isolated and bold on a black background on the screen. The letters were like two feet tall and just right there in my face. I was like, WTF!? I quickly realized that it was the introduction to the movie "Signs" with Mel Gibson from 2002. I happened to turn on the TV and that movie just happened to be starting at that very moment on a randomly selected channel.

I was like, *"OK, that is just weird."* But then when I went to change the channel, it wouldn't change—it was stuck! Something was wrong and the screen wasn't changing no matter which buttons I pushed. I ended up having to restart the TV.

It felt like somehow, my mom was controlling it, making it stay there and making me acknowledge that these were signs from her.

I just stared in shock at the bedroom wall for a few minutes. *"What is going on?"* I kept thinking. *"Mom, is that you?!"* My mind was scrambled. How could this be happening?

. . .

When I first started noticing these "signs," I felt like shouting from the rooftops, "She's still here! I can connect with her! We are communicating! This shit is real!" But then, I would mostly keep it to myself. It sounded unhinged!

Sometimes I feel like Nancy Drew; kind of a dorky, lone woman on a quest to solve a mystery. When I stare at the stars, when I dream, when I notice a little "sign" from the Universe, I am paying attention. I'm trying to figure it all out and it seems to tie in so perfectly with my mom's visions. Her beautiful description of how it all works continues to make sense to me the more I live with it. Meanwhile, I continue to add up each little clue like a puzzle piece, and the picture is filling in.

. . .

These signs I have been experiencing since her death, have reshaped how I look at the world. They have awakened in me an awareness of a connection to something beyond this one life— something beyond just this physical world. I value this new connection. I seek it out, and I hope for more ways to grow more connected to this "other side."

. . .

Could it be that these *breadcrumbs* might be evidence of what she meant by "Will" in the fourth realm? If our deceased loved ones are still intact as energy sources who can have free will, might they try to guide us from [*the beyond*] using things that can feel like signs? This leads me to ask, are these signs evidence of the what some might perceive as an angel or a spirit guide? I have no idea, but I am curious.

As I've shared my experiences with others and have taken more interest in the topic, I have heard many other compelling stories along these same lines. There are millions of fascinating stories of these kinds of spiritual interactions.

. . .

One Sunday morning amid all these new signs I was experiencing, I heard a fascinating story on NPR by reporter Nina Keck.[6]

Keck was interviewing Kris Francoeur, a novelist and middle school principal from Vermont who had lost her son, Sam, in 2013 when he was only 20 years old. Her experience with this terrible loss was so powerful that she wrote a book about it called *Of Grief, Garlic, and Gratitude.* After Sam died, she experienced some significant and notable signs from him that have had a similar impact on her as the signs from my mom have had on me.

I reached out to Keck and she gladly put me in touch with Francoeur so I could hear more about her stories. Francoeur and I connected about these experiences on Zoom and by phone.

A few years after Sam's death, Kris and her husband, Paul, were following their family's New Year's Eve tradition of packing away Christmas decorations. Kris was really missing Sam that night because he always participated in the festivities and always filled the home with laughter and lively energy. After getting it all packed up in the attic, she silently addressed his spirit that night in bed as she went to sleep. *"Sam, I really need a sign from you. A sign that you are still with us."*

Photo courtesy: Kris Francoeur

A photo of Sam Francoeur

After years of signs from him after his death, she feared that at some point, his spirit would move on and they would not have these surreal interactions anymore. The thought of this was unbearable to her.

"I went out the next morning to walk the dog. I always have my cell phone in my pocket. I realized that the phone in my pocket was ringing. I had unintentionally dialed somebody. I yanked out my phone and saw that I had dialed Sam's number accidentally, which was still a contact in my phone, even though we had canceled his phone line months ago. I immediately hung up the call." Kris says she laughed at it and felt grateful for the "sign" that had come from him. She returned to the house from her walk a little bit lighter on her feet, feeling that maybe he was still around.

"Later, my phone buzzed with a text saying it was from Sam, with his icon and photo. The text said, "Who is this?" Kris said she felt nauseous at the bizarre sight of seeing his face and name popping up on her phone in this active way after his being gone for so many years.

She replied to the text: *"My name is Kris...your number used to belong to my son, Sam, who passed away in 2013, and I pocket dialed the number this morning. Sorry for bothering you."*

Kris said her main fear in all of this was that the person on the other end of the conversation, this stranger, would ask her to delete the number from her phone. *"The idea of taking Sam's number off of my phone hurts more than I can express,"* Kris explained.

A few minutes later, she got a text back saying: *"I understand. I lost a child too."*

Whoever got Sam's number after Kris and her husband turned off the phone line, had also recently lost a child. Kris felt shocked to say the very least.

She replied, *"I am so sorry—there is nothing worse in life and you don't ever get over it. What was your child's name?"*

The person replied, *"Sam."*

They both at first thought it was a prank. But the two moms started communicating back and forth, both in shock that the person on the other end of this accidental phone connection had not only also lost a child, but both kids were named Sam. In time, they came to learn that the two Sams knew each other and were friends before each of them died tragically young in separate instances; the families having never met otherwise.

Kris reports:

> *For whatever reason, the two of them decided we needed to connect. I don't know what they were each seeing or knowing, but I feel there were too many weird coincidences in this situation, that I say, yeah, there was some planning going on on their part.*

Over time, the moms became friends and supported each other with their grief. They agreed that the Sams were on the other side, in cahoots, helping get them together somehow, knowing that their mothers could use each other's help.

. . .

"I don't understand how all of this works, but I also have come to understand that that doesn't mean it isn't happening," Kris said.

> *We have come to the conclusion that there are always going to be things in our lives and the Universe that we don't understand. But that doesn't mean it isn't there. That was a very difficult thing for us to accept in this process and now we have reached a point where something happens, and we have given up fighting it. We now accept that it's happening—and that the veil between the two worlds is maybe very, very thin. We can't explain it, but here it is.*

This experience and many more signs from Sam have led Kris to believe in the power of these forces. She describes this in her book with such eloquence:

"We've come to the conclusion that with an energy force as strong as Sam, the energy has to survive somehow," Kris noted.

Kris said before she lost a child, she wouldn't have believed in that kind of thing, but that's changed.

> *One of the things I have come to accept over these last months is that there are things that I don't fully understand, but that 'forces' are at work.*[7]

> *I felt the beginning of the understanding of how infinite love is, how it doesn't die when*

> *someone's heart stops, and that if you can find your way through the haze of pain, you can still see signs of that love and you can bring good out of your pain.*[8]

Kris and her family at times struggle with grieving the terrible loss of their son at such a young age, but they still look for and enjoy signs from Sam, which bring them some relief from the sharp edges of that pain.[9]

...

I still experience signs from my mom. I haven't talked to many people about them, and there are several instances I've never shared with anyone, even with Ben and the kids. Sometimes they feel too personal. These experiences keep me feeling close to her energy, and her spirit. I'm still learning from her. I'm still experiencing her love in new and interesting ways. No matter if it's all in my head, or it's real, whatever it is brings moments of joy into my grief.

As I wrote this book, I awoke one morning and remembered my dream in which I was in my childhood home; my dad was at the sink in the kitchen and my mom was cleaning the counter. When I walked in, she dropped her rag, came right over, and embraced me with the biggest, warmest hug. I felt a buttery warm love in her soft arms, her slow attention, nothing more important to get to. Just a long, open-armed mother's hug. I felt like it was from her, from the other side. Or, maybe it was just a dream. But either way, I'll take it.

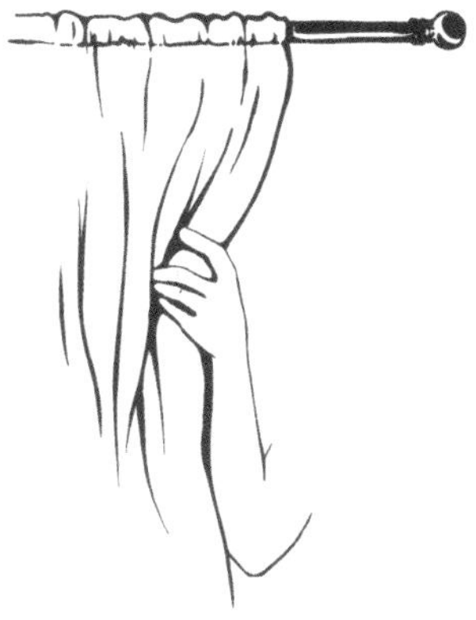

HUMAN INSIGHT

Because I have had these experiences with my mom, I am left wondering—how much can we know? How much can we truly learn about the "other side"? Is it impossible to know what lies *beyond* before we die?

Are these breadcrumbs possibly clues to the reality behind the curtain? And just how close are we to figuring out something more concrete than what science and religion have offered so far over the past few thousand years of human history?

With the connections we now have to one another on the Internet, people are curing diseases, solving problems with life hacks, and sharing solutions. On YouTube, you can learn how to build a bridge, make a peach cobbler in five minutes, or install a new toilet. You can learn how to play any song you can think of, learn how to clean a deer carcass, or follow a newborn bald eagle as it takes its first flight. It's incredible. I mean, yes, we all must endure boring pictures of people's dinners for some reason, and, of course, there are darker sides to it as well. But amazingly, we now have the ability to communicate together collectively and instantaneously. We're in the middle of an incredible advancement in the modern human age.

I love the Netflix series Diagnosis. It showcases "crowd thinking" by allowing people from all over the world to contribute ideas for medical diagnoses that can help solve people's rare and strange health problems. Someone writes in with a set of symptoms after they've been told by their local doctors that there is nothing wrong with their health, or that nothing can be done to change their symptoms.

But through the show, the subjects are connected to an international group of people and scientists. Through these connections, they often find another person who has gone through the same thing or a doctor who has seen this rare set of symptoms. Things like this are saving people's lives through our common connections, our collective thinking, and our collective knowledge. We have proven to be quite an impressive species when we put our collective minds to something.

It's tempting to think of this era as being a pinnacle of technological advancement. But what if we are actually living through a time our descendants will see as primitive? What if the state of our hive-like connection and the power it can wield are just getting going? Is it possible that we could somehow harness this ability, our knowledge, and our energy collectively to break through to something even more significant—something more spiritual, and existential?

Consider how far we have come in our understanding of how we got here, how the Universe works, and the scientific breakthroughs of even just the last century. We have doubled our life expectancy in just a few hundred years. We have figured out the logistics of the solar system, and we are starting to have a presence on Mars. We have built giant cities that shine and sparkle with industry and momentum. We have made incredible art and music, we have gone to the moon, made movies, and built self-learning robots. We have cured diseases, battled wars, and rammed our way through to the present, generation by generation.

And, here we are.

...

What comes next, at least regarding technology and the reality we will live in, is going to be mind-blowing in every way to those of us who had our feet on the ground back in the 20th century. Maybe with all this advancement, we can open our minds to learning more about our fate.

Things advance and change exponentially, and we are all along for the ride, without much of a tangible or reliable understanding of what happens after we die. Despite all these advancements, despite how sophisticated we like to think that we are, we all still have the same fundamental question I had when I was in the fourth grade: *What's happening to all these people we love who are dropping dead all around us?*

. . .

In the series *Surviving Death*[10], Christopher Kerr, MD, PhD, talks about his experiences with patients over the years. He is the CEO and chief medical officer of Hospice & Palliative Care Buffalo and has cared for patients at the end of their lives and their families for decades. In other words, he is an expert in death and dying.

When asked if he believes in the afterlife, he answered:

> *My natural bias is to avoid any questions of spirituality. I would never see a medium or have my palm read or anything. But I think you would be a fool to have seen what I have seen for 20 some years and heard what I have heard, and not think there is more to this story. It's remarkably short-sighted to hang on to this notion that we can only believe what we can see.*

. . .

Humans have been trying—through religion, science, drugs, therapy, self-help books, and countless other avenues—to discover or explain what happens when we die. What happens to our energy, our soul, our "being"?

Consider the possibility of knowing more—not just guessing or scientific conjecture. What if we can gain insights that fill in the shadows that religion and science have yet to explain? What if we can shed light on those dark corners and learn more about the point of all of it, our afterlife, and our place in the Universe?

What if there are truths interwoven in our religions and our scientific explanations and folklore from past generations? What if we need to merge them and mesh them and evolve them to accommodate these new experiences? What if we can grow these ideas into a deeper understanding of the answer to the most fundamental question, *"What is going on here?"*

What if we can get closer to understanding the bigger picture as we continue to advance, generation by generation? Is it possible that we can attain certain glimpses of the true nature of how things work, what happens to us after we die, and the way it is all connected? Can we glimpse behind the curtain? Can we see through the veil, as my mom claimed to at the very end of her life?

THE ANSWER IS "YES"

Just kidding...I don't know the answers to those tough questions.

When my mom was telling me so passionately about her visions of how it all works, she mentioned that we will be asked questions along the way as we advance up through the levels of the funnel-like structure. Specifically, she said when we pass from the knowledge level to the spiritual level, we will be asked some questions. When we are asked these questions, *"the answer is 'Yes,'"* she insisted. She said, *"Certain paths lead to certain questions."*

She said we would be asked questions in some form or fashion as we make progress toward [*the beyond*]. She stumbled when she tried to describe the first question to me. It seemed like it was right on the tip of her tongue, but it was just out of reach, like trying to remember a dream after you awaken, but you can't quite put your finger on it. It almost seemed like something was intentionally preventing her from telling me.

She said the question was related to something such as *"Do you believe in miracles?"* but she said that was not exactly it. She struggled to be able to translate it from the spirit realm into words to share with me.

Months after her death, I found that she had left several voice memos on her phone from that morning where she was trying to figure it out and trying to communicate it, but she just couldn't put it into words. She stuttered and mumbled, getting frustrated by not being able to articulate the first question.

...

When trying to tell me about it, she said, *"The first question that is asked must be answered in the affirmative"* before you can move forward.

Continuing to speak to me along these lines, she said, *"There is some deeper Force that has told you what to answer."*

In a related conversation, she went on to describe that everybody in our current universe has answered "yes" to living in this time and place. *"We have all elected to be here,"* she emphasized. She elaborated that the creation and continuation of our universe depended on this *"opt-in"* type of process and everyone currently living in our reality has chosen to be here. I still find this element of her visions compelling, to say the least. If each of us chose to be here in this body, at this time, how does that change how we live our lives? How does that change our perspective, or our goals?

. . .

To be honest, I don't know exactly what she meant by all of this, but I feel compelled to share it here along with her other insights.

I'm left with so much curiosity about what she meant about these "questions" we might be asked. Who is asking them? Why does it matter? When will we know? What if we don't think the answer is "Yes"?

Losing her has left me wondering and searching for more answers. I wish I'd had another few days, weeks, or years with her to ask more questions about all of it.

. . .

Without her here physically, I seek out and appreciate the signs from her. I feel at ease and comforted by the hope that these visions have brought to me, and meanwhile, I continue to seek the truth.

I'm still in the dark. But I see light coming through some cracks in the surface. There is a new presence, a new power behind the darkness that I didn't know before. I seek its light, its warmth, and the knowledge and peace within it.

IMAGINE

During my mom's last days, as mentioned earlier in this book, she focused much of our conversation on *the ability* to see what she was seeing. *"At the end, you can see ALL of it!"* she exclaimed more than once with excitement.

She emphasized that ***the ability*** to see shapes in the clouds (to be able to interpret something concrete from something abstract) was the same skill that it would take to understand our spiritual reality. This type of thinking would be necessary to understand the structure that she was witnessing, of which we are all a part.

Looking back at it now, I wonder if practicing or trying to see shapes in the clouds (and other similar creative leaps) is a way

I tend to believe that everybody is creative.

– David Byrne, Musician[13]

for us to open certain parts of our brains. Can it maybe kick-start some intangible parts of our consciousness? Is that possibly the path to accessing unused or under-utilized brainpower?

I'm not the only one to wonder about this. Several experts and studies showcase the importance and impact of our creativity.

...

Shelley Carson, PhD[11], explored the concept of creativity in her national best-selling book *Your Creative Brain*. Her cutting-edge research on creativity and the brain is fascinating.

Like most people, she had assumed that some brains are more creative than others. But the more she researched it, she discovered that physically, we're all wired to be creative. She found that some people are better able to access the creative processes in their brains.

Carson said:

> *We're all creative. There are genetic influences...that allow some people to access specific brain activation patterns more easily. When I originally started my inquiries into creativity, I thought that there were creative geniuses and then there were the rest of us. The more you*

> *study the brain, the actual physical brain, the more you realize everybody has the creative hardware, but some people find it easier to access it.*[12]

Carson believes that creativity is not a special secret sauce that only certain individuals have, but rather a basic skill that, if tapped, can help people succeed. She also notes that it can be improved if exercised:

> *Creativity is the ability to produce work or ideas that combine or recombine elements of information that are stored in our brains or that are coming in from the outside world in novel and original ways that have a purpose. Creativity is really important today. If you're going to survive and thrive in this rapid-change climate of the 21st century, you really have to hone your creative capacity.*

...

Perhaps creativity is much more important, much more inherently and deeply critical to our advancement and our understanding than we have ever imagined.

...

The recent docuseries *The Mind Explained: Creativity* explores the idea that it's a myth that some people are more creative than others.

> *We tend to mythologize [artists]. We think they are different from us, somehow driven by madness or blessed by some secret gift. But creativity isn't mystical. It's more like a muscle, and there are ways to train it.*

And, apparently based on the latest research, the whole left brain/right brain dominance theory is also a myth! Creativity doesn't reside in a separate or distinct part of the brain. Rather, it results from the connection of the different parts of the brain. The connection itself creates that spark.

> *Creativity emerges when different regions [of the brain] talk to each other. In the brains of highly creative people, these networks [in your brain] are more connected—they talk to each other more.*

If we are to try to progress up this tornadic, funnel-like structure as my mom insisted, it seems that we need to look for shapes in the clouds more. We need to do more activities that use and train our brains in that way. We need to employ our

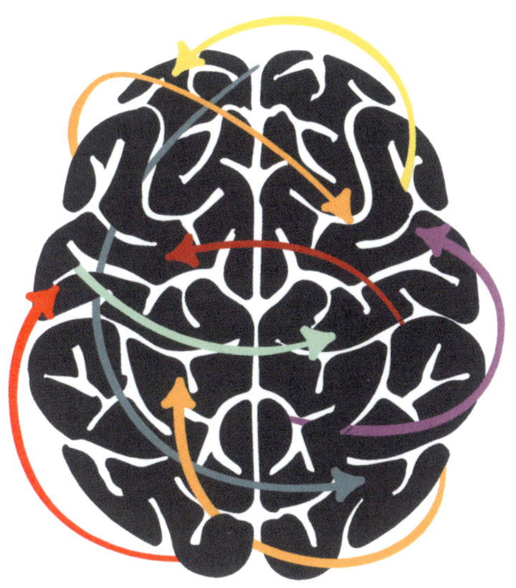

creativity, explore our imagination, and ignite our brains' interconnectivity to advance.

As our brains develop, we learn to conform as part of the natural onset of adulthood, and some people phase out that part of their creativity, associating curiosity and imagination with childishness.

Most artists I know seem to cherish that feeling of "childish" curiosity. According to my mom (and Shelley Carson, PhD), *everyone,* not just artists, can get back to that child-like, wild-eyed perspective to explore and employ their creativity.

In the show, the creators suggest several things that can help a person be more creative, including:

- Allowing yourself to daydream more
- Letting your unconscious take over your active brain more
- Playing games or telling stories that involve your imagination
- Working or creating something without fear of failure
- Sleeping well
- Taking a walk
- Having a general attitude of openness

I asked my good friend Rachel Wyatt to describe what she's learned from staying creatively engaged. She is an artist with several different, always-evolving media and artistic outlets. Rachel replied:

> *To me, being creative means many things—it's about being a problem solver, [having] a growth mindset, open to the possibilities of the unknown...yes, even that unknown. Making art, using our brains in that way, is the expression of parts of our creativity, and should be*

completely honest. To foster curiosity, to help heal deep wounds, to celebrate, to intuit, [we create] because we can.

Be kind. Love your process, no matter what comes out of it. For after all, does it matter to be judged for a week, and not make anything, or to do/be/make and constantly surprise yourself with your kaleidoscope of growth? What you learn when you flex your creative muscles will fan across all areas of your life. It will enrich you and teach you something new constantly.

. . .

My mom focusing our conversation on seeing shapes in the clouds was kind of funny to me at the time. Like, *"What does that have to do with anything, Mom? You are talking about the afterlife, and you are maybe dying in a hospital. Why are we talking about shapes in the clouds?"* But she insisted it was that same type of skill that she was employing to see what she was seeing on the "other side." She was using the "shapes in the clouds" to act as a metaphor to help me understand the brain function of *creativity* that was so critical to her new perspective.

ON THAT NOTE

Music relies on and utilizes the same interconnections between various regions of the brain as other creative endeavors.

My mom's love of music sprang from a well deep inside her soul. She wrote music in the shower, on the plane, and in line at the grocery store. She would *dream* music and would wake up desperately searching for a pencil to write it down, to capture it before it was lost.

Music poured out of her, and she couldn't have stopped it even if she had tried. It saved her life when she was sick, it saved her mind when she needed peace, and it was integral to the person she was. It connected her to God, to nature, to friends, and to herself.

. . .

When I was a kid, I always loved listening to her playing her piano with such grace and beauty. Mom was truly masterful. After she got sick and almost died in the 1980s from kidney disease, listening to her play the piano took on more complexity for me. I realized that one day, she would be gone and I would not be able to hear her play. The threat of losing her to disease started when I was in second grade. Because of that, when I listened to her play, I always tried to soak it in, savor it, live in that specific moment, and hear every little note.

. . .

One afternoon in my mom's final days in the hospital, I was playing a Chopin playlist on my Bluetooth speaker thinking it would lighten her mood and serve as a distraction from her pain. She asked me to turn it off and added, *"You know, honey, there is already so much music playing in my head."*

. . .

Since she's been gone, I have found huge amounts of solace in music. Sometimes it keeps me sane when I feel like my world is falling apart. Finding the right song at the right time has helped me cope with life's crazier moments—especially during the pandemic.

I honestly don't know how I could have been able to process this loss, this grief, without it. Listening to the music my mom composed and performed is more meaningful than when she was alive. But I also feel compelled to explore music in general, listen to it with intent, and fill my mind with it when I need to escape, focus, relax, or settle into certain types of work.

I'm not the only one. Research shows that music has huge benefits to our mood, our brain development, and maybe something more spiritual or even eternal.

. . .

On my mom's office wall, she had a poster titled "5 Reasons Why Music Boosts Brain Activity."[14] It is an article specific to Alzheimer's patients, for whom music plays an increasingly critical role in modern-day treatments. Here are five reasons listed in the online article about why researchers believe music boosts brain activity:

1. Music evokes emotions that bring memories.
2. Musical aptitude and appreciation are two of the last remaining abilities in dementia patients. Music is an excellent way to reach beyond the disease and reach the person.

3. Music can bring emotional and physical closeness. Dancing can lead to hugs, kisses, and touching which brings security and memories.
4. Singing is engaging. Singing activates and connects different parts of the brain. Singing leads to many more activated visual areas of the brain, exercising more mind power than usual.
5. Music can shift mood, manage stress, and stimulate positive interactions.

Even though these principles are geared toward Alzheimer's patients, they all apply to healthy brains as well.

. . .

Music is sometimes called the universal language because it transcends so many of our differences. Music creates a common experience that we all can share. It's a special thing with a little bit of magic in it: it's more than just the black notes on the page or an app on your phone or a plastic CD that skips. Music is an energy that transcends the physical world.

In my mom's office, she had several different posters, photos, and quotations all over the walls. These were things that inspired her and she loved them. Here is a photo of one of them that is a framed needlework by an unknown author.

In one of my favorite podcasts, Short Wave, science reporter Rasha Aridi explained some of the neuroscience behind music and the brain.[15] She interviewed Keith Doelling, a postdoctoral researcher at the Institut de l'Audition in Paris, France. His specialty is the neuroscience of speech and music perception.

Doelling talks about music's ability to trigger many different things in us—rhythm and physical movement, emotion, memory, and singing. He says:

> *Because so many different parts of our brain process music, our memories of music are also stored away in different parts, too. So, if you can, you know, remember looking at a piece of sheet music, that memory is coming from the visual processing center. Or if you can remember a dance, that memory is coming from the cerebellum that houses your muscle memory.*

Music connects all these various parts of the brain in unique ways that we don't fully understand yet. Music triggers and interconnects more parts of the brain than almost any other kind of brain activity.

Life contains a great deal of beauty and happiness but also tragedy, heartache, and pain. Because of its "full brain" integration, is it possible that music has a way of helping us process and release the harder feelings in life, like grief and loss?

Perhaps music can provide an escape route for negative emotions to leave or release from our brains. It might be exactly what we need when we are struggling. For many, it can be an effective medicine for the soul.

Here is how my mom felt about music:

Music Is…

Music is the magic garden
where my mind comes to play.

It is the grassy plain
over which my imagination
gallops unbridled.

It is the gentle breeze
which carries the wings of
my hopes to the heavens.

It is the sandy beach
where my thoughts giggle
with cool, wet, gritty delight.

It is the ocean tide
whose lilting cadences set the
pace for my own heart.

It is the trysting place
where my soul pours out
its secret longings.

It is the love-bed
where my dreams may
frolic unreproached.

– Carlie Burdett

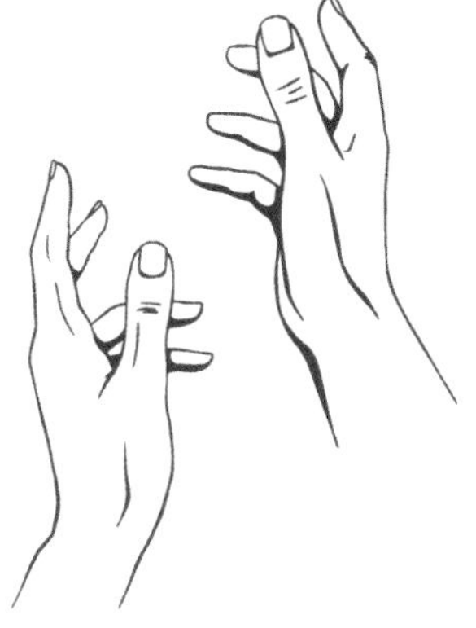

LOSS

Sometimes I feel Mom all around me. I feel her influence on my choices and I hear her voice in my head. One thing I have learned about processing my grief is to follow it where it leads me. To *go there* when I need to. This brings light to the darkness, and a tiny bit of joy begins to grow where the grief has settled.

Of course, losing my mom leaves me sad that she is gone, but also, I'm grateful for the gifts she has given me. All of it leaves me wishing for others to find that same peace, especially those in the painful throws of loss or tragedy.

. . .

"The grieving process can look very different from person to person," says Mary Frances O'Connor, PhD, associate professor of psychology at the University of Arizona, where she directs the Grief, Loss, and Social Stress (GLASS) Lab. *"The range of emotions is wide and varies quite a bit[16]."*

She points out that grief produces a wide spectrum of emotions at different times: panic, sadness, yearning, difficulty concentrating, confusion, and more. *"It isn't something that you get over. It becomes a part of who you are. It becomes a part of how you understand the world,"* she says.

> *When we have the experience of being in a relationship, the sense of who we are is bound up with that other person. The word 'sibling' [and] the word 'spouse', imply two people. And so when the other person is gone, we suddenly have to learn a totally new set of rules to operate in the world.*

She continued, "*I really think of grieving as a form of learning. And the background is running all the time for people who are grieving.*"

...

My grief comes in waves and always lives in the background each day. At first, I would have a really good cry most mornings after the kids left for school, and anytime I could get away for a night alone, which seemed more important now. My grief would build up and, at first, I could only go a few minutes or hours without crying and being overwhelmed by the pain. Then, I could go a few days, then weeks. It seemed to build up though, almost like a hunger for food, or a thirst for water. It seemed physical, building over time.

Now, I'll recognize it and sometimes I can see it coming days or hours in advance. And, then, other times, it just appears out of nowhere. Bam! Something can randomly trigger my grief, and I'll burst into tears, sometimes dropping a "cry bomb" on whoever is around, usually my husband, Ben.

One day, right after work, I was doing laundry and complaining to Ben about how much I hated all my bras. I didn't even realize he was paying attention, but before I knew it, he had his phone hooked up to the TV and was pulling up images of bras on a website, asking me what features I liked and didn't like. Smack! Unexpected grief wave. I burst into tears, completely surprising not only myself but Ben, too.

When you lose the one you love...
It's not somethin' you get over...
But it's somethin' you get through...

– Willie Nelson

It hit me with grief because when Ben offered his help I realized that my mom was the one who had always helped me buy bras. His helping me in that same way triggered the realization that I had never bought a bra without her in all my 44.5 years.

Small things like this seem to be popping up constantly and unexpectedly in my daily activities.

...

Of course, there have also been more serious moments of sadness in grieving my mom. About six months after she passed, I was overcome by her absence during a time when I knew that I needed to stop drinking and take better care of my health. I needed to start sleeping better. I knew I needed to change. I needed help.

More than ever, I needed more energy to meet the challenges my life required: a full-time, demanding job where I was accountable to my clients and employees; and, my vital role as a mom to two energy-zapping kids (love 'em). I also had a marriage to maintain, a spirited one-eyed cat, a rambunctious, very large puppy, a few needy chickens, a bearded dragon, and a partridge in a pear tree. And in the middle of all of that, I also felt compelled to find time to breathe. I needed big changes in my life, and I desperately wanted my mom's help with all of it.

But she wasn't here. I couldn't call her. I couldn't melt my feelings into words over the phone to her or cry them into tears onto her shoulder. So, I did the next best thing I could think of. I went to the graveyard, sitting by her tombstone explaining all the things I needed to change. I wept openly on her grave, kneeling in the dirt, acknowledging that I couldn't do it on my own. I needed her help. I begged her for wisdom and strength.

Grief is like the ocean; it comes on waves ebbing and flowing.
Sometimes the water is calm, and sometimes it is overwhelming.
All we can do is learn to swim.

– Vicki Harrison

Many people don't talk about grief and loss because it makes them feel vulnerable, weak, sad, embarrassed, anguished, or awkward. We tuck it all away. This seems to be especially true in American culture. We don't want to bother or burden people with "negative" feelings. We sweep grief under the rug. We box it up so others don't see our discomfort and sorrow.

. . .

"We don't die well in America," Anthony Bossis, PhD, says in Michael Pollan's book *How to Change Your Mind*. *"The biggest taboo in America is the conversation about death.*[17]*"*

Sometimes it seems that we are so afraid—so collectively afraid—of loss and even of grief itself. Sometimes it feels like we are so afraid of dying, that we don't even live. We have a long way to go in terms of understanding death, dying, and being willing to try to heal our fears. I believe we are in the middle of an ongoing existential crisis collectively and individually. Perhaps that is the reason the world seems so dark these days.

On Glennon Doyle's podcast, *We Can Do Hard Things,* the topic of death comes up when the podcaster interviews the author Ashton Applewhite,[18] who wrote the book *This Chair Rocks: A Manifesto Against Ageism*. On the podcast, Applewhite talks about how important it is to talk about dying.

> *We don't want to think about getting older, we don't want to think about dying. We are aging from the minute we are born. It's not something annoying that old people do. Dying is a discrete biological event at the end of all of that living.*

. . .

"We need to normalize death and grief," my good friend David Wyatt so wisely explained to me. *"We need to have a modern conversation about dying."*

David was only 27 when he lost his dad and has been processing and living with grief for the past 20 years. He said:

> *There's this prevalent idea that we don't want to say the wrong thing about death, dying, and grieving. So, many people just say nothing, which makes the process needlessly isolating and puts distance in family, friend, and even professional relationships where there could be support and closeness.*
>
> *Naturally, that's rooted in cultural norms and fear—about death itself or causing further hurt. But my observation is that it is also an outcropping of the notion that grief will pass within a few months or a year at the longest.*
>
> *In truth, we don't move on from grief as much as we move on with it. It changes who we are and how we see the world around us. That is intimidating for people because so many [people] value sameness and normalcy. The sense of impermanence is fundamentally unsettling for some [people] so they avoid the topic. But as Robert Frost wrote in his poem A Servant to Servants: "...the best way out is always through."*

David continued:

> *While not everyone is equipped or inclined to face death directly and really sit with those emotions, I would argue that death, dying, and grief are every bit as beautiful and as much a part of life as birth, love, family, and career. In fact, the aching sorrow of death is what gives the elation of childhood or new love or healing their meaning. It's the contrast that makes life beautiful and worthwhile.*

...

If my mom's visions and the journey that she described to me are true, then the fear of death and dying is not necessary. What if we could become more comfortable with death, dying, and grief?

My good friend Alex Meyers is a hospice volunteer and an end-of-life doula-in-training, meaning that she helps people and their families during the dying process, the way a doula helps with birth, but with the end-of-life transition. She believes that if we can more deeply embrace the concept of death, the transition can be much easier, even beautiful. She recalls:

> *When I was in my 20s, my mother died, and she spent her last weeks in a hospice facility. She had spent several weeks before that in the hospital, and the shift to hospice was wonderful in many ways—a much more peaceful environment that was supportive of family members, and staff that was more attuned to her comfort and who took the time to explain to us what was going to happen.*
>
> *Though cancer had already metastasized by the time she was diagnosed, I can't recall her or any family member mentioning anything about death or dying to each other, even when she was obviously careening towards the end. It had struck me then as deeply weird and disturbing that no one was talking about the elephant in the room. Though I think my family was on the extreme side of the 'denial' spectrum, I don't think this attitude is that uncommon in this country.*

Alex was inspired to go into hospice care to help dying people and their families deal with death better than her family did. She told me:

> *I want to help...the dying person transition as smoothly and painlessly as possible. I also want to help loved ones grieve authentically and learn how to most skillfully incorporate their loss into their lives moving forward.*

I asked Alex what she thinks is wrong with our approach to death and dying in America.

> *Let's start with the medical field—medical schools barely discuss death in physician training. This is slowly changing, but the medical attitude overall is still that death is the enemy, that death is [a] failure.*
>
> *To deny the truth of the inevitability of death is to deny ourselves and our loved ones the agency to make the experience as comfortable, authentic, redeeming, and yes, as beautiful as it can be.*

...

Not being in denial, and being able to have more open conversations about death and dying might allow us to live in less fear, and to be able to support one another better in our times of need. It could help us with our own fears as well. Fear of death does not have to linger over all of us.

Thích Nhất Hạnh was a Vietnamese Buddhist monk and peace activist. This "Zen master" published hundreds of books and studied comparative religion at Princeton University. He died on January 22, 2022, at the age of 92 after a long life in which he shared beautiful revelations and insightful wisdom. He wrote about the loss of his mother and how he still felt her presence in a powerful and compelling way after she died:

> *The day my mother died I wrote in my journal, "A serious misfortune of my life has arrived." I suffered for more than one year after the passing away of my mother. But one night, in the highlands of Vietnam, I was sleeping in the hut in my hermitage. I dreamed of my mother. I saw myself sitting with her, and we were having a wonderful talk. She looked young and beautiful, her hair flowing down. It was so pleasant to sit there and talk to her as if she had never died. When I woke up it was about two in the morning, and I felt very strongly that I had*

never lost my mother. The impression that my mother was still with me was very clear. I understood then that the idea of having lost my mother was just an idea. It was obvious in that moment that my mother is always alive in me.

I opened the door and went outside. The entire hillside was bathed in moonlight. It was a hill covered with tea plants, and my hut was set behind the temple halfway up. Walking slowly in the moonlight through the rows of tea plants, I noticed my mother was still with me. She was the moonlight caressing me as she had done so often, very tender, very sweet...wonderful! Each time my feet touched the earth I knew my mother was there with me. I knew this body was not mine but a living continuation of my mother and my father and my grandparents and great-grandparents. Of all my ancestors. Those feet that I saw as "my" feet were actually "our" feet. Together my mother and I were leaving footprints in the damp soil.

From that moment on, the idea that I had lost my mother no longer existed. All I had to do was look at the palm of my hand, feel the breeze on my face or the earth under my feet to remember that my mother is always with me, available at any time.

– Thích Nhất Hạnh[19]

. . .

Since my mom passed, I have had times where I strangely feel closer to her than when she was here physically. She is all around me, in my head, and ever-present. Her energy flows freely in a way that is more accessible to me now, more a *part* of me.

Of course, I'd prefer a phone call. And I would trade my right arm for one more hour with her, but I am trying to adjust and be open to this new type of connection.

NIGHTFALL AND STARSHINE

Since my mom passed away, I feel an urgent and powerful need to connect with nature. Experiencing nature has significantly helped me in my grief. It makes me feel like I can breathe, connects me to her, and helps me feel closer to her.

One of my childhood friends, Cody Wilson, shared that my mom's curiosity and interest in nature had always made an impression on him. When we were kids, his family owned and operated a small farm on the outskirts of the small Texas town where we lived. He said he remembered that one time my mom called his mom and asked if she could stop by to listen to the wind blow through their wheatfields. Connecting to nature helped my mom throughout her life in different ways.

...

I have come to believe that the natural world is one big living organism, and we are all a complex and beautiful part of it. I believe that experiencing and interacting with the natural world is not only helpful to us but necessary. We are a part of it as much as it is a part of us—I believe that it is not only natural but *critical*.

Science writer Sonia Shah wrote about this interconnected relationship between humans and the natural world in her best seller, *The Next Great Migration*[20]. She talked about our connection to nature and how we are interconnected with the natural world in a Fresh Air podcast in 2020[21]. She described how natural migration is for our species, and how mixing with various plants, animals, and microorganisms leads to very positive outcomes. She talked about how moving around in general benefits most species, including ours.

Look deep into nature, and then you will understand everything better.

– Albert Einstein

Shah believes, *"It's all tied in with our health and how well we thrive or don't thrive."*

"Our health is connected to the health of animals and livestock and the planet itself," she attests.

. . .

Ming Kuo, an environmental psychologist at the University of Illinois Urbana-Champaign has been conducting biological research on the effect of nature (especially trees) on our mental and physical well-being for well over a decade. In a 2022 interview with Aaron Scott[22], she discussed her findings of scientific proof that there is a huge amount of biology behind how our bodies and minds respond to our environment. Apparently, just as we might have been intuiting for a long time, science can now prove that being in nature makes a huge difference in all our physical and mental systems.

As part of Kuo's research, she took blood samples before and after walks in nature by the study participants. She was surprised to find that the blood chemistry of the participants changed significantly and repeatedly, even accounting for controls of other variables.

Kuo shares:

> *What we know is that nature seems to be tied to a huge array of health outcomes. So if you live in a greener area you are less likely to have diabetes or heart disease or mental health disorders, muscular issues, [or] skeletal issues.*

Being in or seeing nature and natural things (trees especially), makes our bodies feel genuinely relaxed. This exposure to the natural world has a blood-test-proven calming effect on our brains and the chemical balances in our bodies.

Kuo adds:

> *Some of the plausible pathways between contact with nature and health involve short-term physiological and psychological effects, which, if experienced regularly, could plausibly account for long-term health effects.*

Her research shows that regular exposure to nature helps individuals:

- Cope better with big decisions
- Have more impulse control
- Have better cognative functioning
- Get along better with others
- Boost their immune levels more than double
- Experience reduction in Attention Deficit/ Hyperactivity Disorder (ADHD) symptoms
- Experience reduced depression and anxiety disorder
- Fight off various infectious diseases

- Fight off certain types of degrees of cancer
- Heal from surgery
- Loose weight
- Have better birth outcomes
- Fight cardiovascular disease, musculoskeletal complaints, migraines, respiratory disease, and others

The list goes on and on and on.

Hearing or seeing water, looking at or having exposure to trees, smelling natural smells like flowers and other plants—experiencing these kinds of things regularly helps our bodies feel calm and allows them to build up a higher immunity baseline in addition to other things. It gives you overall better health—both physically and mentally.

And, her research shows that regular exposure to nature helps more than just individuals. It also helps larger groups collectively. Nature and green spaces help communities:

- Get along better
- Have fewer instances of violence
- Be overall safer
- Have better academic achievement

Communities with greenery and green spaces generally have large health, social, and academic advantages.

Unfortunately, there is a huge discrepancy in access to nature across human communities. Kuo points out that low-income areas have very little tree cover compared to higher-income areas. *"You can even see from space which areas have tree cover and green spaces and the differences are smack-you-in-the-face obvious,"* Kuo relates.

Kuo's research shows that even seeing smaller elements of nature in city life are beneficial. A green view from your window, seeing trees on your walk to work, or being able to see the sky can all greatly increase your general health and happiness. Gardening or visiting a park also helps boost these levels of happiness and calmness. Ming argues that planting trees should be one of the next big public health interventions. *"Just like we decided having indoor plumbing was a good idea, I think having trees for everyone is a good idea."*

Kuo reports:

> *Trees tend to make us our better selves, not only in terms of our physical well-being and functioning but also our social and cognitive well-being and functioning. Trees are a necessary part of a*

healthy human habitat. Where there are trees, we see people smarter, kinder, healthier, and stronger in every imaginable dimension.

. . .

Since losing my mom, spending time in nature makes me feel more alive and more connected to life. I crave it and want more of it.

When I was a kid, I spent a lot of time playing in rivers and being outside among the trees, birds, and bugs. Now, I crave nature because it reminds me of childhood adventures and makes me feel alive in a whole different way. I seek it out as often as I possibly can, even if it's just a quick walk between work meetings. My clever little seven-year-old niece, Lucy, recently said that I "talk to nature." It struck me because it's not something I've ever heard articulated in that way.

Of course, "nature" is a pretty broad term. There are lots of specific things in the natural world that help me feel connected to my mom. Birds (especially chickadees, of course), trees, and sunsets are prime examples. When I watch nightfall come and witness those changes in the sky, I feel like I'm experiencing a light show that I can't stop watching.

. . .

But maybe more than anything, it's the stars that get me.

I always loved seeing them as a kid. Who doesn't? But especially in my grief, I can't seem to get enough of them. Watching them recharges me like a phone plugged into the wall. It feels restorative to my very core. It feels like a drug that entices me and connects me to the future and the past, while somehow allowing me to be in the present more than ever before.

...

The human connection to the stars is long and deep. In *The Real Book about Stars*[23] (my grandmother's stargazing guide, which was passed down to me by my Aunt Donna) author Hal Goodwin begins the book by saying:

When you go out of doors on a clear night and look up at the sky, you are doing something that [humans] have done for countless thousands of years.

The stars soon become old friends, just as they've been the silent friends of man for countless thousands of years.

...

World famous astrophysicist Carl Sagan disrupted our understanding of our place in the Universe when he said in 1980 during his TV show *Cosmos*, "*The cosmos is also within us. We're made of star stuff. We are a way that the cosmos can know itself.*"

When he said we are made of star stuff, he wasn't just being metaphorical. He meant that the atoms of nitrogen in our DNA, the calcium in our teeth, and the iron in our blood were all forged in the interiors of stars[24]. We are made of the same stuff as the stars. No wonder we feel a connection!

. . .

Jo Marchant, PhD, an award-winning science journalist, speaker, and a New York Times bestselling author, explores the nature of humanity and our universe, including the awe-inspiring power of the night sky.

In her latest book, *The Human Cosmos: Civilization and the Stars*, Marchant explores the impact stargazing has had on human civilizations and the importance of our connection to the wonder of the night sky[25].

On the KERA podcast *Think*, Marchant described to the guest host, John McCaa, the experience of stargazing[26]:

> *Just looking at it, or even just looking at a photo of it, will make you more creative, more curious, happier, and less stressed, more connected to*

other people, more generous, less materialistic, and would help you feel as if you have more time. That is exactly what psychologists have found.

They have found that the starry sky is one of the most powerful sources that we know of the emotion of awe—the feeling of something that is vast, that dwarfs you, that is beyond you. When psychologists want to trigger awe, they show pictures of the stars. It changes our outlook on life.

Awe improves our well-being. People make more ethical decisions. They want to help others. They care less about money and more about the planet. Experiencing the sheer vastness shifts our focus from our daily concerns and connects us to a bigger picture.

. . .

So, it's not just me! It was reassuring to find this research because especially after my mom passed, I started noticing how the stars made me feel more connected, healed, loved, and energized. They compelled me to keep going, even when things were hard. I searched for and found this star research *after* I had become completely obsessed with them.

One night early in my grief, Ben and I were stargazing. It got late, and Ben went to bed. But, I watched the stars until well after midnight. The starshine felt like a drug that I just couldn't pull myself away from. Something about it felt immensely healing, especially amidst this huge loss. I craved basking in their sparkle and mystery for as long as possible. There was something in those stars that felt compelling in a deep and primal way. I still crave them and seek them out as often as possible.

DAWN

When my son Henry was only a few weeks old, Ben and I often lied down with him on a little patch of grass behind our way-too-small rental house and looked up at the big, old oak trees. We knew he couldn't see all the details of the leaves, but at his little infant stage, he could detect light and dark. He could distinguish between the contrast, and he loved it so much. It would mesmerize him, and he'd become calm and happy, even entranced by it.

As he aged, Henry, of course, became able to distinguish more than just between lightness and darkness. He was more keenly aware of the shapes of leaves in the trees, and he could observe more detail than just light and dark blobs.

A year or two ago, Henry, Ben, and I found ourselves lying under a tree looking up again, and we told Henry about those early days 16 years ago when he had viewed the oak trees in our yard when he was a baby. We told him about how much he loved it. It made me think about how much he's changed, how much detail he can see now, not just in the leaves and branches of the tree above us, but about life, our family, me, and himself.

As we age, we see more and more granularity in life. I'd argue that children see the world in black and white. Clean and simple. But as we go through life and grow older, we notice more nuance and complexity.

As I come to terms with my mom's visions and try to understand them more fully, I think about this trend of growth and progress. As we live our lives over and over, we make progress up the structure, one life at a time. And, as we do this, we learn more and more. We learn more about the details of our existence and our spiritual reality. As we rise up through the different stages of the funnel, the resolution of our spiritual reality gets sharper and sharper until one day, we can see it with complete clarity just as my mom did in the days before she passed.

...

I believe based on what my mom relayed to me that we have multiple lives to learn and grow from our mistakes as we cycle upward toward [*the beyond*], the fourth realm. And, in these numerous lives, we experience things over and over in various ways until we learn specific lessons.

But how do we learn those lessons? How do we ensure we are moving upward and making progress, rather than being static or going backward (if that is even possible)? How might we advance? What are the commonalities that can help us progress upward and onward through these levels?

In this world, these days, we are all in demand 24/7—glued to our screens, shutting off multiple alarms or reminders every second, raising our kids, trying to make a living, dealing with traffic, and oh yeah—the pandemic, climate change, and the general "cluster clump" (as my niece Lucy would say) of it all. How are we even supposed to have hope for each simple day here on Earth, much less clue into signs from the Universe to advance on a spiritual journey?

We have been in the dark for so long about why we are here and what the point of life is. We have dreamt of enlightenment, and we have witnessed those who have had brushes with it. We can see the light and dark blobs in the distance, but how do we sharpen our senses? How do we refine the resolution to see a clearer picture? How do we as a species, groping in the dark, find our way and start seeing this reality for what it is?

I believe we must find the light within ourselves. We must find that same light we connect with when we see the stars. I think the same starlight lives within us and is an electric energy that lives at our core—our *root* energy, our spirit.

Perhaps my mom's reference to the Dawn is about our hidden, inner light needing to emerge, whatever color, texture, or shape it might be. Maybe it's an emergence of a spark inside of you that can rise, out of the darkness, just like the morning Dawn, giving birth to the true you, the true light inside of you, the same light that has always been inside of you and always will be. The light is you—not your physical body in the year 2024 or 2056 or whenever you are reading this—but the true, eternal, spiritual you.

Dawn is connecting with our inner light, connecting with the stardust that made us and the stars that guide us. Dawn is the light inside of you, rising to meet the challenges of each new day.

What makes you shine? What makes you happy? This is your internal light—this is your dawn. Sing your song. Bang your drum. Let your light shine.

. . .

OK, I know...all of this sounds corny-as-hell at best, and absurd at worst, but that's how I've come to understand my mom's intention in wanting to call this book of hers *Dawn*.

What are the implications of my mom's visions? If this "spiral-up-through-various-levels toward oneness" vision is

If everything fails, start over. Failure is not fatal. It's inevitable that you learn from your mistakes.

If you fail, you start over. If you fail again, you start over again. If you fall seven times, get up eight...

You will pass some and fail some, but the ones you fail you will remember longer.

Kind of like in life, you keep coming back till you get it right.[27]

– Willie Nelson

anywhere close to the truth, then it necessarily indicates reincarnation. And how does that impact how we live our lives and how we make our choices on a daily basis?

I think if this reincarnation-up-the-spiral situation is real, then I think "practice makes perfect" may apply. Repetition and learning might be the key, just like my very strict piano teacher used to say. Try, fail, learn. Repeat. Try, fail, learn. Repeat.

...

I've been watching the dawn from time to time, since my mom passed away. It was the least I could do since it was the name of the book she was supposed to write about these visions.

My mom always had a particular affinity for the dawn. She talked about it, wrote about it, and composed music about it. I think she saw it as a magical time of the day. "You never know what the day might hold!" she would say in a sing-song, clichéd mom voice.

. . .

To be honest, I don't know if *this* is what she had in mind when she described a book called *Dawn* to me. Honestly, I don't even know what to make of all this—her visions, her references to the dawn, the answer being "Yes"...I struggle with not knowing more, not knowing the details; I struggle with not having more time to ask her all the questions that I have.

All I know for sure is that all of this has made me more curious about our journey. More than ever, I am seeking the truth. We'll never find it if we don't look for it.

. . .

I believe that my mom's visions give us a partial glimpse of something larger than ourselves. Yes, these moments with her and the insights she described were personal to me and to her, but I believe that there is something universal in them, a greater truth about the human experience we all must face -- a truth that is worth examining. I believe that her visions of the nature of our existence offer an alternative to living in fear of death; an alternative to living in fear, in general.

My mom emphasized to me during those special last few days that life itself is inherently based on searching and striving. Her visions paint a picture of striving toward betterment, striving for progress, and striving together toward love and connection.

Our mission is to simply *try*. Try to use the best paths and follow the best forces we can find to help us make progress upward and onward. This journey focuses on seeking health and knowledge, finding spirituality, and, ultimately, becoming a part of [*the beyond*].

. . .

Dawn is hope. Dawn is a new beginning. Even when things are the lowest, even when things are terrible, hold on for the dawn. Hope for it; look forward to it; wait for it.

Each day, the dawn offers a fresh new start, an opportunity for a new perspective.

Dawn is the optimist inside of you, shouting at you to look up, put your shoulders back, take a deep breath, and put one foot in front of the other.

Dawn is momentum.

Dawn is enlightenment and transition.

Dawn is your quiet moment in peace.

Each day, the dawn calls for us to continue to rise up and strive toward the future, knowing that, as my mom put it, ***"There is nothing to be afraid of."***

Photo by: Jennifer Lindberg

EPILOGUE

More About Carlie Sue Hunter Burdett

Carlie Sue Hunter Burdett's life story is one of love and devotion to her dear husband Tom, to their children Bliss, Shannon, and Dorie, to their five grandchildren, and to her faith, music, friends, and community. She leaves us with music that continues to bring joy, tears, humor, and dignity to our lives in her absence. Carlie generously shared her many talents, her deep well of compassion, her natural grace, her sweet spirit, and her passionate energy with us all.

Carlie Sue Hunter was born to Mayme Powers Hunter and J. Marvin Hunter, Jr, in Baird, Texas, on May 2, 1946. The youngest of four children, Carlie's father was a Texas historian and newspaper publisher, and her mother was a school teacher. Carlie worked alongside her family in their printing business, where she learned to write, proofread, and do production layout. Carlie grew up with a love of letters, history, and geology. Her parents, her Aunt Lettie, and her siblings Dolores, Jack, and Elmyra shared a deep connection with music, poetry, and art.

During her childhood, the family moved to Grand Prairie, Texas; then to Buffalo, Wyoming; and finally to Kerrville, Texas, where Carlie graduated from Tivy High School. In her

youth, she studied piano, sang in school and church choirs, twirled a baton, and excelled in schoolwork.

While she was in high school, she spent summers working as a substitute secretary for their church, and in her leisure time, she enjoyed the Guadalupe River with friends. An influential person in her life was her grandfather J. Marvin Hunter, Sr. She loved to visit his Frontier Times Museum in Bandera and listen to his stories about different times and cultures. Carlie attended Abilene Christian University for one year before transferring to The University of Texas at Austin, where she majored in music.

Her love story with Tom began in Kerrville, Texas, in 1963. Their love and partnership inspired her life throughout the following years as students at The University of Texas, followed by the next many years as residents of the Texas Panhandle. Carlie taught piano and music theory, and enjoyed being a mother of three.

Carlie and Tom were partners in private and public life—Carlie as spouse to Tom at events for his law firm, Tom as spouse to Carlie at her musical performances, and for each other at their church and in charitable, and civic leadership roles.

The happy progress of their lives was interrupted in 1987 when Carlie became ill with ongoing migraines and other symptoms. After several months of searching for answers

Photo by: Kelly West

from various doctors, Tom and Carlie decided to go to Scott & White Hospital in Temple, Texas, for a diagnosis. Within a couple of days, her condition was identified as an autoimmune disease called Rapidly Progressive Glomerulonephritis (RPGN) that was adversely affecting her kidneys. She underwent a kidney biopsy, followed by chemotherapy and steroid treatments for RPGN. Thankfully, after several months of treatment and many prayers, the condition was controlled and she resumed a normal life for several years, enjoying grandkids and other joys of her life.

But in 2000, some lab work, followed by another kidney biopsy, showed a potential problem. This time, the diagnosis was Focal Segmental Glomerulosclerosis (FSGS), and there was no treatment for her except for eventual dialysis or a kidney transplant. However, the disease was moving slowly. She had another three years of a fairly normal life before she needed dialysis.

In 2003 when Carlie's kidneys failed, her husband, Tom, donated one of his healthy kidneys through a transplant to Carlie, giving her another 16 years of precious life, health, and sweet partnership.

Carlie's love of music helped carry her through years of illness and wellness. She could play any requested song by ear at occasions ranging from weddings to Christmas gatherings to playdates with grandchildren.

Carlie composed hundreds of sacred and secular musical works, some of which will remain available on her website, carlieburdettmusic.com. She created music based on her passions for math, poetry, song, and piano to develop a distinctive composition style, informed by her extensive study of composition methods and inspiration from her life and those around her.

Carlie's Christian faith was central to her life and fueled her creative energy. She was thankful to God for every valuable gift and offered her music as a celebration of life and an encouragement to people dealing with problems and stresses in their lives.

Carlie is survived by her husband of 53 years, Tom Burdett; daughter Bliss Burdett; son Shannon Todd Burdett; daughter Dorie Burdett Pickle and her husband, Ben Pickle; like-a-son Erik Ringen of Oslo, Norway; grandsons Erik Allen Burdett and Thomas Blake Burdett; granddaughter Hanna Carlie Pak; and grandsons Henry Duke Pickle and George Marvin Pickle. She is also survived by her brother Jack Hunter, sister Dolores Farrell, and many cousins, nephews, and nieces.

Carlie passed away peacefully on Thursday, August 1, 2019, at Baylor Scott & White Hospital in Temple, Texas, surrounded by her family while her treasured music played in the background.

Remember the Mountains

Written for my dad in 1964 (when she was about 18 and they were falling in love).

Sharon's Song

Written for Bliss in 1971 (when she was about one year old).

Shannon's Song

Written for Shannon in 1990 (when he was about 18).

December's Child

Written for me in 1983 (when I was about 7 years old).

Waiting for the Dawn

Written many years before her passing.

My Song

Written by Carlie for herself in 1992 (when she was about 46); Also the song that played as she passed.

ACKNOWLEDGMENTS

I want to thank so many people for helping me with this book. I could not have done it without so much love and support in my life.

I thank my husband, Ben, for being so patient and supportive during my unconventional grieving process of decorating animal skulls, writing amateurish songs on my flute, and escaping for overnight excursions to make time to grieve and also to create this book. He is my best friend, my confidant, and the best partner a person could dream of or hope for. He always knows just what I need and gives the best hugs humanly possible. Ben, I hope to find you in each of my lives.

I'm grateful for my older son, Henry, for always questioning everything, challenging my theories, and being so naturally curious. You amaze me. I love you and your genuine, unique self. We are more alike than you may think.

I thank my younger son, George, for being a kindred spirit to me on this journey—for seeing the shapes in the clouds alongside me. I love you. You inspire me, and I know you will live your life to the fullest.

(And, I thank both of you for understanding my disappearing now and then to grieve and to write.)

Thank you, Dad, for the privilege of your guidance throughout my life. You have always been there for me, guiding me, showing me the way, and protecting me. I remember your playing whoopsie-daisy with me on the living room rug as a young, happy child; I remember your warm hug and practical advice when you left me at college for the first time. I remember your walking me down the aisle on that cold rainy night at my wedding. You have always shown me how to live my best life not only through your admirable example but also through your kindness and love. You have been so supportive and encouraging, and for that, I am the luckiest girl in the world. Thank you.

Thank you, my big brother, Shannon. You have made me tough, and I've come to appreciate it. What kid isn't gonna be tough when her brother nicknames her "Dorky" and teaches her how to wrestle, fish, and play football? You have always supported me and loved me, even when I was an annoying little sister. We share a common energy, you and I, brother. Your enthusiasm and your smile light up any space. Keep your light burning bright. I love you.

And, I thank you, my sister, Bliss. You are beautiful inside and out. I have always followed your example and your advice throughout life because I have always loved, trusted, and admired you. You have shown me what a total badass looks like. You have pushed me outside of my comfort zone repeatedly with appreciated results. I don't know where my life would be without you.

And I thank my in-laws, Jan, Gary, Lori, and Jeremiah, who continue to give me so much love and unconditional support. I am so grateful to be a part of your family. I couldn't imagine my life without you all.

Thank you to my nieces, Lucy and Hanna, who both inspire and impress me constantly. Thank you to my nephews, Erik, Thomas, and Charlie—each of you is unique and amazing. To the five of you, keep being true to yourselves, and the world is your oyster.

Thank you to my friends who contributed to this book whether it was through encouragement, contributing your quotes, or your feedback. I couldn't have done it without you.

Special thanks to Cate Berry, Jodi & Owen Egerton, Jennifer Fahrenbacher, Kris Francoeur, Kim Karrasch, Ava Swan, Shanny Lott, Reilly Magee, Brianna McKinney, Alex Meyers, Lori Privitera, Nancy Reynolds, Jason Richard, Diane Tyler, and David & Rachel Wyatt.

Thank you for believing in me and helping this come to fruition as my mom envisioned.

Thank you to the doctors and nurses at Baylor Scott & White (BSW) Hospital who cared for Mom during her final stay and throughout the years, helping protect her transplanted kidney so she could stay with us as long as possible. Thank you, BSW, for advancing medicine and evolving healthcare forward.

I thank each of my grandparents who have guided me from the other side—I look to the stars as often as I can in gratitude for you.

And, last but not least, I want to thank my mom, who inspired and informed this book. Thank you for your lifelong dedication to genuine love and connection. Thank you for showing me how to stop and look life right in the face. Thank you for showing me the path forward.

ENDNOTES

1 Kalanithi, Paul. "When Breath Becomes Air" New York: Random House, 2016.

2 Berry, Katherine. "The Ladder." [Date and publication source unknown.] Author's note: This poem by Katherine Berry is printed on a card given to me by my parents for graduation from graduate school. I have kept the card taped on the wall next to my desk for the past 20 years. It inspires me daily.

3 Fogelman, Dan (producer). *This Is Us,* [Television series]. Los Angeles: Rhode Island Ave. Productions, Zaftig Films, and 20th Century Fox Television, season 2, episode 18: *"The Wedding,"* 2018.

4 Dvorsky, George. "15 Uncanny Examples of the Golden Ratio in Nature." 20 Feb. 2013, Gizmodo [Website], https://gizmodo.com/15-uncanny examples-of-the-golden-ratio-in-nature-5985588.

5 Micalizio, Caryl-Sue. National Geographic Society; 20 Nov. 2012 [Website] https://mindmatters.ai/2022/03/unexplained-maybe-unexplainable-numbers-control-the-universe.

6 Keck, Nina. "'Our Moms Have to Talk'; Pocket Dial Connects Grieving Moms." Vermont Public Radio, 22 Jan. 2020, www.vermontpublic.org/vpr-news/2020-01-22/our-moms-have-to-talk-pocket-dial-connects-grieving-moms.

7 Francoeur, Kris. *Of Grief, Garlic, and Gratitude: Returning to Hope and Joy from a Shattered Life: Sam's Story.* New York: Morgan James Publishing, 2019, p. 203.

8 Ibid., p. 229.

9 Francoeur, Kris. [Website]: https://authorkfrancoeur.com.

10 Conceicao, Jonele, Ricki Stern, Jesse Sweet, and Jessica Vale (producers). *Surviving Death* [Television series], New York: Break Thru Films, episode 5: "Seeing Dead People," 2021.

11 Carson, Shelley. *Your Creative Brain: Seven Steps to Maximize Imagination, Productivity, and Innovation in Your Life.* San Francisco: Jossey-Bass, 2012.

12 Powell, Alvin. "Harnessing Your Creative Brain." *The Harvard Gazette*, Mar. 2011, https://news.harvard.edu/gazette/story/2011/03/harnessing-your-creative-brain.

13 Moore, Julianne, David Byrne, Heather Berlin, and Faith Jones (performers). *The Mind Explained* [Television series], Washington, DC: Vox Media Studios. episode 4: "Creativity," 2021.

14 Sauer, Alissa, "5 Reasons Why Music Boosts Brain Activity." [Website] Alzheimers.net, www.alzheimers.net/why-music-boosts-brain-activity-in-dementia-patients, 2014.

15 Aridi, Rasha, and Rhitu Chatterjee. "Why Music Sticks in Our Brains." *Short Wave* [Podcast], 7 Oct. 2021, NPR, www.npr.org/2021/10/05/1043417378/why-music-sticks-in-our-brains.

16 Kwong, Emily. "What Happens in the Brain When We Grieve." *Short Wave* [Podcast], 8 Nov. 2021, NPR, www.npr.org/2021/11/04/1052498852/what-happens-in-the-brain-when-we-grieve.

17 Pollan, Michael. *How to Change Your Mind: What the New Science of Psychedelics Teaches Us About Consciousness, Dying, Addiction, Depression, and Transcendence,* New York: Penguin Press, 2018, p. 404.

18 Doyle, Glennon. "Pro-Aging: Why the Best is Yet to Come with Ashton Applewhite," *We Can Do Hard Things* [Podcast], episode 81, 25 Mar. 2022, https://momastery.com/blog/we-can-do-hard-things-ep-81.

19 Hạnh, Thích Nhất. *No Death, No Fear: Comforting Wisdom for Life.* New York: Riverbook Books, 2002, pp. 4-5.

20 Shah, Sonia. *The Next Great Migration: The Beauty and Terror of Life on the Move.* New York: Bloomsbury Publishing, 2020.

21 Davies, Dave. "Rethinking the Migration of All Living Things," *Fresh Air* [Podcast], 2 June 2020, NPR, www.npr.org/2020/06/02/868163560/rethinking-the-migration-of-all-living-things.

22 Scott, Aaron. "Good Things Come in Trees," *Short Wave* [Podcast], 21 June 2022, NPR, www.npr.org/2022/06/15/1105229060/good-things-come-in-trees.

23 Goodwin, Harold Leland. *The Real Book About Stars.* Garden City, NY: Garden City Books, 1951.

24 Greenfieldboyce, Nell, and Emily Kwong. "The Curious Stardust at the Ocean Floor," *Short Wave* [Podcast], 26 May 2021, NPR. www.npr.org/2021/05/24/999940229/the-curious-stardust-at-the-ocean-floor.

25 Marchant, Jo. *The Human Cosmos: Civilization and the Stars*. New York: Dutton, 2020.

26 McCaa, John. "For Inspiration, Look to the Stars," *Think* [Podcast], 18 Dec. 2020, KERA. https://think.kera.org/2020/12/18/for-inspiration-look-to-the-stars.

27 Nelson, Willie. *Roll Me Up and Smoke Me When I Die: Musings from the Road*. New York: William Morrow, 2021, p. 29.